Longman English Interactive 3

Activity and Resource Book

Michael Rost

Longman English Interactive 3
Activity and Resource Book

Acknowledgments
We wish to extend our sincere appreciation to Victoria Badalamenti, Elizabeth Ianotti, Jennifer Benichou, and the students of the English Language Center at LaGuardia Community College for inspiring the concept of this Activity and Resource Book. Additionally, we wish to thank the following users, reviewers, and piloters of *Longman English Interactive* for contributing ideas toward the development of the Activity and Resource Book:

Elizabeth Ianotti, Jennifer Benichou, *LaGuardia Community College*
Banu Yaylali, Kathy Biache, *Miami-Dade Community College*
Alfredo Rodriguez, *KPMG Mexico*
Julie Fanara, *Howard Community College*

The author wishes to thank Kathleen Field, Nancy Blodgett, Lynn Contrucci, Hugo Loyola, Irene Frankel, and Sherry Preiss for their guidance and support during the development of this activity book. The author also wishes to thank the entire Pearson multimedia team for their ongoing development of *Longman English Interactive*.

Pearson Education, 10 Bank Street, White Plains, NY 10606

Cover design: Inez Sovjani
Cover photo: Mark Harmel/Stone (Getty Images)
Text design: Quorum Creative Services
Text composition: TSI Graphics
Illustrations: Kenneth Batelman
Photo credits: **page 10** © A.K.G., Berlin/Superstock; **page 11** © Bettmann/CORBIS;
    page 54 (*left*) © Royalty-Free/CORBIS; (*right*) © (277984), Profolio Enr./IndexStock

---

LONGMAN ON THE **WEB**

Longman.com offers online resources for teachers and students. Access our Companion Websites, our online catalog, and our local offices around the world.

Visit us at **longman.com**.

ISBN: 0-13-152086-5

Printed in the United States of America
1 2 3 4 5 6 7 8 9 10–WC–09 08 07 06 05

Contents

Scope and Sequence

Module	Video Listening	Vocabulary	Speaking	Grammar	
A.1 **Another Busy Day**	Predict relationships. Listen for facts and main ideas about people's lives.	Words related to how you feel	Make social plans. Accept and decline invitations.	• Contrast: simple present and present continuous • Expressions for suggesting • Infinitives with *too* and *enough*	
A.2 **Breaking News**	Predict people's actions. Listen for information about events and main ideas about people's intentions.	Words related to the concept *authentic*	Tell someone news or gossip. Respond to news or gossip.	• Present perfect for indefinite past • Modals of advice • Future with *will* and *be going to*	
A.3 **A Job for Talia**	Predict people's actions. Listen for information and the speaker's intended meaning in conversations.	Pairs of nouns and adjectives	Propose an idea. Convince someone to let you do something.	• Contrast: present perfect and simple past • Modals of ability • Possessive pronouns	
A.4 **A Matter of Trust**	Predict conversation topics. Listen to understand people's relationships and feelings.	Idioms with *take*	Confirm that you know someone. Respond to someone who recognizes you.	• Tag questions • Adjectives and adverbs • Articles: *a, an, the*	
B.1 **Nick's Explanation**	Predict people's intentions. Listen to understand people's reasons and beliefs.	Idioms with *get*	Give orders and make requests. Respond to orders and requests.	• Non-action verbs • Modals of request • *So* and *such*	
B.2 **Bad News**	Predict how people will solve problems. Listen to understand reports of events and people's judgments.	Expressions with *feel*	Make statements about possibility. Ask about possibility.	• Gerunds as subjects and objects • Modals of possibility • Reflexive pronouns	

Task Listening	Pronunciation	Reading	On the Web	Writing
Listen to an excerpt from a journalism class lecture and complete notes.	• Stress in words • Rhythm in sentences	An article about workaholism	Research how 2 companies are keeping their employees happy.	Write a descriptive paragraph about how one company is attracting employees.
Listen to a short biography on TV and order events.	• Reduced vowel sounds • Rising intonation for some questions	An article about interesting soccer facts	Research popular sports.	Write a descriptive paragraph about a sport.
Listen to voicemail messages and take notes.	• Falling intonation for statements and *wh-* questions • Stressed and unstressed *do*	An interview with a singer about how she got her big break	Research some popular celebrities.	Write a short biography of a celebrity.
Listen to an announcement for a TV series and fill in a TV schedule.	• Focus words • Intonation for tag questions	An article about class reunions	Research 3 companies that help people plan reunions.	Write a descriptive paragraph about the services a company offers.
Listen to advice on a health website and put the instructions in order.	• Stressed and unstressed words: *can* and *can't* • The vowel sounds in *play* and *let*	An article about sports injuries with tips on safety	Research sports and their most common injuries.	Write an expository paragraph about common sports injuries.
Listen to callers on a radio talk show and match their opinions to their pictures.	• Loss of the *h* sound in pronouns • The vowel sounds in *stop* and *just*	An interview with a news reporter on how to write a good news story	Research news websites.	Write a summary of facts.

Module	Video Listening	Vocabulary	Speaking	Grammar	
B.3 **An Endorsement Deal**	Predict people's reactions. Listen for background details and for ideas about people's reasons.	Pairs of verbs and nouns	Respond to news. Ask follow-up questions.	• Past continuous • Modals of preference • Comparative adjectives	
B.4 **No One By That Name**	Predict events. Listen for specific events in a story. Understand humor.	Words related to *yell*	Express certainty and uncertainty. Confirm facts.	• *Used to* • Embedded *wh-* questions • Indefinite pronouns	
C.1 **No Help for Nick**	Predict what someone knows. Listen to understand descriptions and people's ways of solving problems.	Idioms related to the expression *cheer up*	Ask and give permission. Offer help. Accept and decline help.	• Past continuous with *when* • Modals of permission • Comparisons: *as* + adjective + *as*	
C.2 **In the News**	Predict the contents of a news report. Listen for details of a problem and for people's hidden meaning.	Inseparable phrasal verbs	Ask for and give opinions.	• Inseparable phrasal verbs • Gerunds and infinitives • Future time clauses	
C.3 **The Truth Revealed**	Predict events. Listen for advice and for people's intentions.	Idioms with *out of*	Express necessity. Ask questions about necessity.	• Infinitives of purpose • Modals of necessity • Participial adjectives	
C.4 **Dean's Challenge**	Predict people's reactions. Listen to understand relationships and people's reactions.	Separable phrasal verbs	Ask for and give clarification.	• Present perfect continuous with *for* and *since* • Separable phrasal verbs • Superlative adjectives	

Task Listening	Pronunciation	Reading	On the Web	Writing
Listen to TV ads and put the last line of the jingles in order.	• The *er* sound in *soccer* • The voiceless *th* sound in *think*	An article about endorsement deals	Research celebrities and the products they endorse.	Write an expository paragraph about a celebrity and the products he/she endorses.
Listen to people's conversations with a receptionist and find the offices they are asking about.	• Unstressed words: *of, at, for, to* • Reduced phrases: *used to*	An article about anger management	Research websites that teach how to manage anger.	Write about your opinion.
Listen to a fashion show and put the models on the catwalk.	• Unstressed words: *as* • Linking words together: consonant to vowel	An article about how to avoid identity theft	Research websites of organizations that help victims of identity theft.	Write an expository paragraph about what a victim of identity theft should do.
Listen to a TV chef and put the ingredients on recipe cards.	• Stress in phrasal verbs • Reduced phrases: *going to*	An article about naming traditions	Research naming customs and traditions around the world.	Write a comparison/contrast paragraph about naming customs.
Listen to news about a soccer player's new contract and fill in the contract details.	• Reduced phrases: *have to, want to, got to* • Pronunciation of *-ed* endings	An article about how to negotiate cross-culturally	Research websites about customs and traditions around the world.	Write a comparison/contrast paragraph about cultural traditions.
Listen to a coach's speech about motivating players and put the slides in order.	• Consonant clusters • Intonation showing surprise	An article about how body language shows whether someone is being honest	Research websites about body language.	Write an expository paragraph about the meaning of gestures and expressions in different cultures.

To the Teacher

About *Longman English Interactive*

Longman English Interactive is a comprehensive multimedia course that lets students work at their own pace on a range of language learning activities. *Longman English Interactive 3* consists of software (two CD-ROM disks) that students use in a computer learning lab or on their own computers. Each unit is based on a scene from an ongoing video story, with closely linked exercises for listening, speaking, grammar, pronunciation, vocabulary, and reading development. Each unit of the CD-ROM course provides up to 4 hours of self-paced instruction employing extensive video, audio, and animated graphics, and including interactive exercises, review quizzes, and immediate feedback.

About the *Longman English Interactive Activity and Resource Book*

This *Activity and Resource Book* is designed to serve as a personal or classroom resource for learners and a management tool for teachers and course coordinators who are using the *Longman English Interactive* multimedia software.

- Simple screenshots help students quickly learn how to use the software.
- Progress Checks for each unit enable students to keep a record of completed activities and scores on the review quizzes in the CD-ROM course.
- Additional listening tasks let students review the course audio segments. Each *Activity and Resource Book* includes an audio CD.
- Expanded grammar exercises for each grammar point allow students to consolidate learning.
- Vocabulary reviews offer students new ways of remembering key words and phrases from each unit.
- Language Functions exercises give students additional controlled practice with the functional language expressions from the unit.
- Application Activities provide multiple ways for students to apply what they have learned in realistic ways.

This *Activity and Resource Book* can be used as a self-access learning guide or as a classroom text for students who are using *Longman English Interactive*. Best used after completing each unit of the *Longman English Interactive* CD-ROM course, students can use the *Activity and Resource Book* at home, in the computer lab, or in the classroom. Students can complete each exercise (Listening, Grammar, Vocabulary, and Language Functions) on their own or with a study partner or group and consult the Grammar Explanations at the end of each unit of the *Activity and Resource Book* as needed. They can also refer to the Audioscript, a glossary of vocabulary terms, and the functional language charts, and they can check their own answers with the Answer Key at the back of the *Activity and Resource Book*.

Classroom follow-up will help students consolidate their learning and allow for additional personal attention. As time permits, teachers can also guide the students with the selection of one or more Application Activities which wrap up each unit. Teachers or course coordinators should be sure to monitor students' Progress Checks, to confirm that students are completing each section of the CD-ROM course and are showing ample progress on the review quizzes at the end of each unit.

For additional classroom communication activities, the *Longman English Interactive Communication Companion* is available as both 12 downloadable documents (PDFs) in the CD-ROM course or as a full 48-page, four-color book. The *Longman English Interactive 3 Teacher's Guide*, available for download on the Longman website (www.longman.com/multimedia), provides further suggestions for classroom activities as well as the Web Research and writing assignments for each unit.

The following chart gives an overview of how the sections of the *Longman English Interactive Activity and Resource Book* correspond to the CD-ROM course.

CD-ROM course section	*Activity and Resource Book* corresponding section
Video Listening 1	Listening Exercise A (with Audio CD): a new activity with the same extract
Video Listening 2	Listening Exercise B (with Audio CD): a new activity with the same extract
Vocabulary	Vocabulary: review of vocabulary items in a new context
Speaking	Language Functions: review of the functional language expressions in a new context
Grammar 1	Grammar 1: a review of the grammar point in a new context
Grammar 2	Grammar 2: a review of the grammar point in a new context
Grammar 3	Grammar 3: a review of the grammar point in a new context
Task Listening	Listening Exercise C (with Audio CD): a new activity with the same extract
Pronunciation	
Reading	
Unit Summary Review Quiz	Application Activities

To the Student

Welcome to *Longman English Interactive 3*. This *Activity and Resource Book* will help you with the course.

After you complete each unit of the CD-ROM course, review the unit by doing the exercises in this *Activity and Resource Book*.

Here is a study guide for using the CD-ROM course.

Start at the Course Home.

- Click on the **Orientation** button to download a PDF file with detailed information about using the CD-ROM course.
- Click on the **Course Overview** button to start the course.

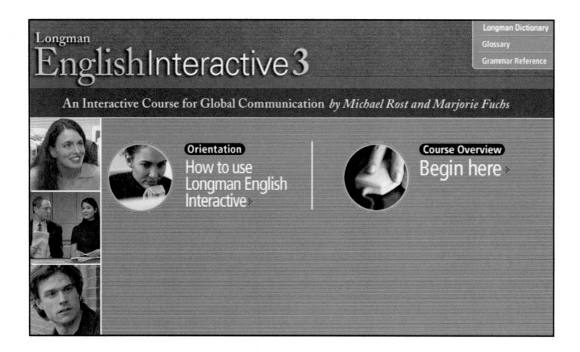

Choose a unit.

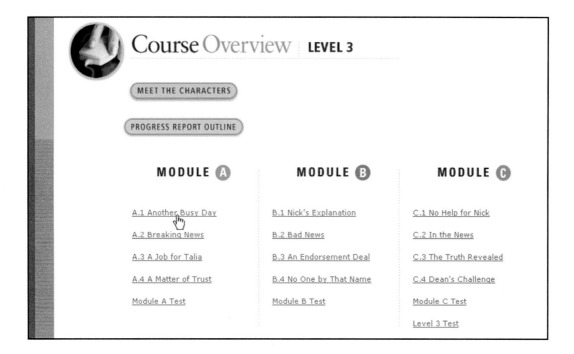

Choose a skill to practice.

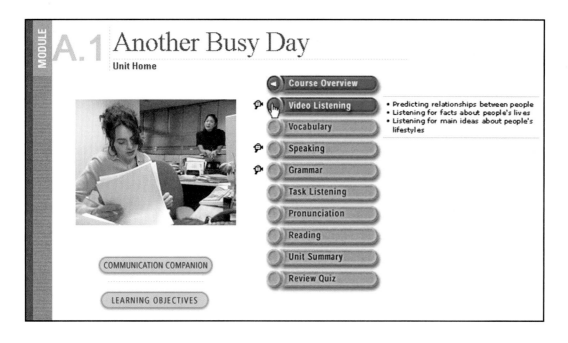

As you go through each unit in the CD-ROM course, try these study tips:

Video Listening

- Watch each video 3 times.
- Use the "pause" button, if necessary.
- Pay attention to the characters' body movements and facial expressions.
- Try the exercises. Check your answers. Click on 🔲 to hear part of the recording again.
- Check the transcript after you finish.

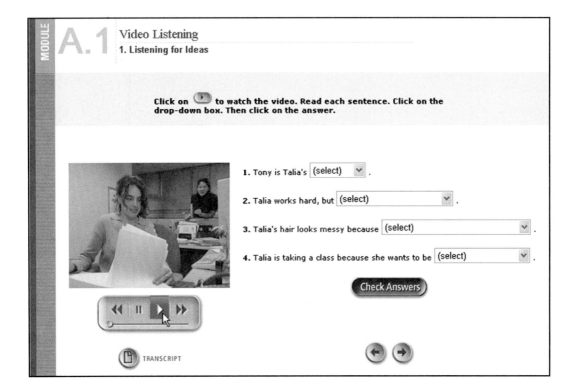

• Click on the Culture Notes button to learn more about how to interpret the characters' gestures, expressions, and intonations.

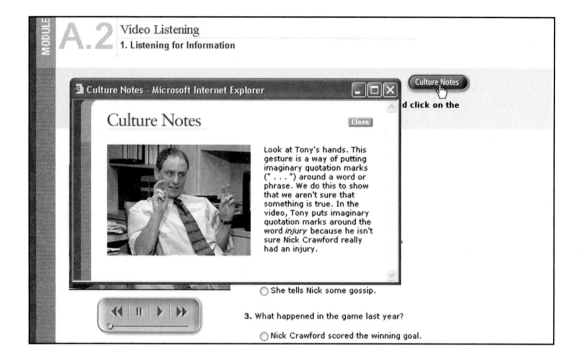

Speaking

- Study the Language Functions charts. Click on ⊙ to listen to the expressions.

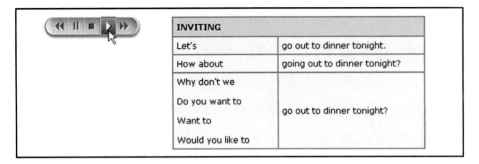

INVITING	
Let's	go out to dinner tonight.
How about	going out to dinner tonight?
Why don't we	
Do you want to	
Want to	go out to dinner tonight?
Would you like to	

- Do the practice exercises.
- Click to the Role Play Introduction page and listen to the sample conversation. Then click to the Role Play page.
- Click on ⊙ to listen to the character from the video. Read the **directions** for hints on how to respond. Listen to the **model** if you need more help.
- Record your voice. Speak loudly and clearly.

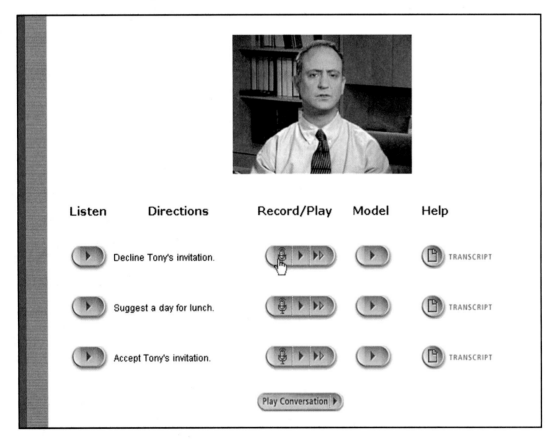

- Play back your voice. Record again if you want.
- Click (Play Conversation ▸) to listen to the entire conversation.
- Try again. This time, use different functional language expressions from the unit.

Grammar

- Listen to the grammar presentations.
- Watch as the words grow, move, and change color. Think about the grammar.
- Use the Grammar Chart and Grammar Help buttons to find out more about the grammar topics.
- Try the exercises. Check your answers. Click on 🄴 for an explanation.

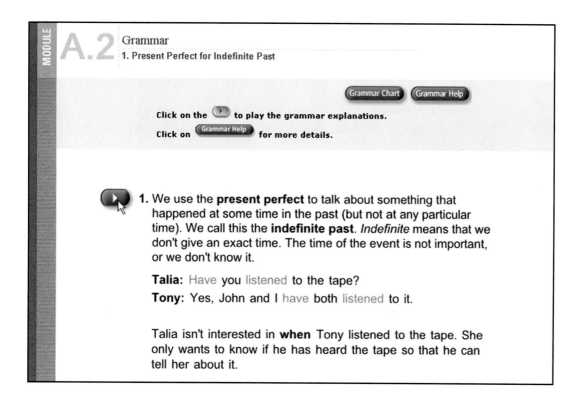

MODULE

A.2 Grammar
1. Present Perfect for Indefinite Past

(Grammar Chart) (Grammar Help)

Click on the ▶ to play the grammar explanations.

Click on (Grammar Help) for more details.

1. We use the **present perfect** to talk about something that happened at some time in the past (but not at any particular time). We call this the **indefinite past**. *Indefinite* means that we don't give an exact time. The time of the event is not important, or we don't know it.

Talia: Have you listened to the tape?

Tony: Yes, John and I have both listened to it.

Talia isn't interested in **when** Tony listened to the tape. She only wants to know if he has heard the tape so that he can tell her about it.

Task Listening

- Click on ⏵ to listen to the recording.
- Use the "pause" button, if necessary.
- Follow the directions to complete the exercise as you listen. You will type in text, click on objects, or drag text from an answer pool on the screen.
- Check the transcript after you finish.

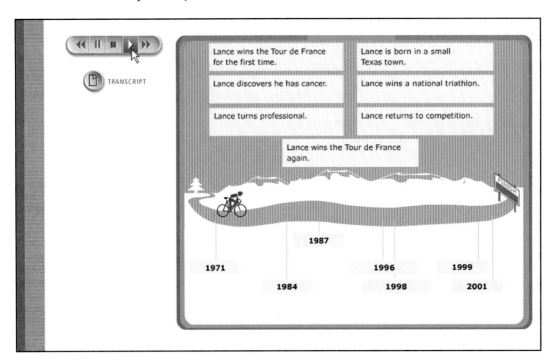

Pronunciation

- Listen to both pronunciation sections and do the practice exercises.
- Record your voice. Compare with the model.

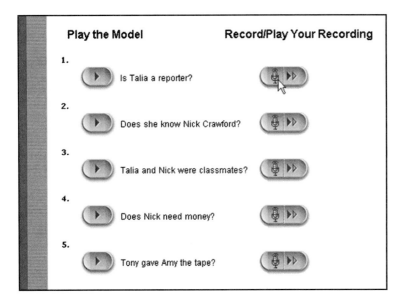

Review Quiz

- Take the review quiz for each unit.
- Check your score. Review the necessary skills if you have any difficulties.

Progress Report

Unit A.1 Review Quiz

Learner's name:

Score: 85%

Language area	Number correct/number of items
Listening for information	6/7
Listening for ideas	2/3
Vocabulary	4/4
Speaking	4/6
Grammar (Simple present vs. present continuous)	4/4

When you use this *Activity and Resource Book*, spend between 50 and 110 minutes on each unit.

Progress Checks

Record your progress for each unit of the CD-ROM course. Make a check (✓) for each activity that you completed. Write your scores for the Review Quiz. (5 minutes)

Listening

Use the Audio CD and do the exercises. (20 minutes)

Vocabulary

Do the Vocabulary exercises. Check the Glossary if necessary. (10 minutes)

Grammar

Review the Grammar Explanations. (10 minutes)

Do the Grammar exercises. (20 minutes)

Language Functions

Review the Language Functions charts.

Do the Language Functions exercises.

Answer Key

Check your answers on pages 123–131. (5 minutes)

Application Activities

Choose two or three activities. Start the activities. (20 minutes— You will need more time for some activities.)

When possible, study with your classmates and your teacher. You can learn a lot of English with *Longman English Interactive*! Have fun using the course.

Name _____   Date _____

A.1 Another Busy Day

As you complete each section of the CD-ROM course, make a check (✓). Write your scores for the Review Quiz.

Video Listening
_____ **1.** Pre-listening
_____ **1.** Listening for Information
_____ **1.** Listening for Ideas
_____ **2.** Pre-listening
_____ **2.** Listening for Information
_____ **2.** Listening for Ideas

Vocabulary
_____ How Do You Feel?
_____ Practice

Speaking
_____ Language Functions: Inviting
_____ Language Functions: Practice
_____ Role Play 1
_____ Role Play 2

Grammar
_____ **1.** Simple Present and Present Continuous
_____ **2.** Expressions for Suggesting
_____ **3.** Infinitives with *Too* and *Enough*

Task Listening
_____ Journalism Class

Pronunciation
_____ **1.** Stress in Words
_____ **2.** Rhythm in Sentences

Reading
_____ Pre-reading
_____ Preview vocabulary
_____ Get a Life!
_____ Comprehension Check

Review Quiz	Score
Listening for information	_____ / 7
Listening for ideas	_____ / 3
Vocabulary	_____ / 4
Speaking	_____ / 6
Grammar 1	_____ / 4
Grammar 2	_____ / 3
Grammar 3	_____ / 3
Pronunciation 1	_____ / 3
Pronunciation 2	_____ / 3
Reading	_____ / 4

A.2 Breaking News

As you complete each section of the CD-ROM course, make a check (✓). Write your scores for the Review Quiz.

Video Listening
_____ **1.** Pre-listening
_____ **1.** Listening for Information
_____ **1.** Listening for Ideas
_____ **2.** Pre-listening
_____ **2.** Listening for Information
_____ **2.** Listening for Ideas

Vocabulary
_____ Is It Authentic?
_____ Practice

Speaking
_____ Language Functions: Talking about News or Gossip
_____ Language Functions: Practice
_____ Role Play 1
_____ Role Play 2

Grammar
_____ **1.** Present Perfect for Indefinite Past
_____ **2.** Modals of Advice
_____ **3.** Future with *will* and *be going to*

Task Listening
_____ This TV Minute: Lance Armstrong

Pronunciation
_____ **1.** Reduced Vowel sounds
_____ **2.** Rising Intonation for Some Questions

Reading
_____ Pre-reading
_____ Preview vocabulary
_____ Fascinating Soccer Facts
_____ Comprehension Check

Review Quiz	Score
Listening for information	_____ / 7
Listening for ideas	_____ / 3
Vocabulary	_____ / 4
Speaking	_____ / 6
Grammar 1	_____ / 4
Grammar 2	_____ / 4
Grammar 3	_____ / 2
Pronunciation 1	_____ / 3
Pronunciation 2	_____ / 3
Reading	_____ / 4

Name _____ **Date** _____

A.3 A Job for Talia

As you complete each section of the CD-ROM course, make a check (✓). Write your scores for the Review Quiz.

Video Listening
_____ **1.** Pre-listening
_____ **1.** Listening for Information
_____ **1.** Listening for Ideas
_____ **2.** Pre-listening
_____ **2.** Listening for Information
_____ **2.** Listening for Ideas

Vocabulary
_____ Nouns and Adjectives
_____ Practice

Speaking
_____ Language Functions: Convincing
_____ Language Functions: Practice
_____ Role Play 1
_____ Role Play 2

Grammar
_____ **1.** Present Perfect and Simple Past
_____ **2.** Modals of Ability
_____ **3.** Possessive Pronouns

Task Listening
_____ Taking Messages

Pronunciation
_____ **1.** Falling Intonation for Statements and *Wh-* Questions
_____ **2.** Stressed and Unstressed *Do*

Reading
_____ Pre-reading
_____ Preview vocabulary
_____ Singer of the Year!
_____ Comprehension Check

Review Quiz   **Score**
Listening for information . . . . _____ / 7
Listening for ideas . . . . _____ / 3
Vocabulary . . . . _____ / 4
Speaking . . . . _____ / 6
Grammar 1 . . . . _____ / 4
Grammar 2 . . . . _____ / 4
Grammar 3 . . . . _____ / 2
Pronunciation 1 . . . . _____ / 3
Pronunciation 2 . . . . _____ / 3
Reading . . . . _____ / 4

A.4 A Matter of Trust

As you complete each section of the CD-ROM course, make a check (✓). Write your scores for the Review Quiz.

Video Listening
_____ **1.** Pre-listening
_____ **1.** Listening for Information
_____ **1.** Listening for Ideas
_____ **2.** Pre-listening
_____ **2.** Listening for Information
_____ **2.** Listening for Ideas

Vocabulary
_____ Take Your Pick 1
_____ Practice

Speaking
_____ Language Functions: Getting Reacquainted
_____ Language Functions: Practice
_____ Role Play 1
_____ Role Play 2

Grammar
_____ **1.** Tag Questions
_____ **2.** Adjectives and Adverbs
_____ **3.** Articles

Task Listening
_____ Shakespeare and His Works

Pronunciation
_____ **1.** Focus Words
_____ **2.** Intonation for Tag Questions

Reading
_____ Pre-reading
_____ Preview vocabulary
_____ Let's Get Together!
_____ Comprehension Check

Review Quiz   **Score**
Listening for information . . . . _____ / 7
Listening for ideas . . . . _____ / 3
Vocabulary . . . . _____ / 4
Speaking . . . . _____ / 6
Grammar 1 . . . . _____ / 2
Grammar 2 . . . . _____ / 4
Grammar 3 . . . . _____ / 4
Pronunciation 1 . . . . _____ / 3
Pronunciation 2 . . . . _____ / 3
Reading . . . . _____ / 4

Name _____ Date _____

B.1 Nick's Explanation

As you complete each section of the CD-ROM course, make a check (✓). Write your scores for the Review Quiz.

<table>
<tr><td>

Video Listening
_____ **1.** Pre-listening
_____ **1.** Listening for Information
_____ **1.** Listening for Ideas
_____ **2.** Pre-listening
_____ **2.** Listening for Information
_____ **2.** Listening for Ideas

Vocabulary
_____ I Just Don't Get It
_____ Practice

Speaking
_____ Language Functions: Giving Orders and Making Requests
_____ Language Functions: Practice
_____ Role Play 1
_____ Role Play 2

Grammar
_____ **1.** Non-action Verbs
_____ **2.** Modals of Request
_____ **3.** *So* and *Such*

Task Listening
_____ Health Web

</td><td>

Pronunciation
_____ **1.** Stressed and Unstressed Words (*can't* and *can*)
_____ **2.** The Vowel Sounds in *play* and *let*

Reading
_____ Pre-reading
_____ Preview vocabulary
_____ Play It Safe
_____ Comprehension Check

Review Quiz   **Score**
Listening for information . . . . _____ / 7
Listening for ideas . . . . _____ / 3
Vocabulary . . . . _____ / 4
Speaking . . . . _____ / 6
Grammar 1 . . . . _____ / 4
Grammar 2 . . . . _____ / 4
Grammar 3 . . . . _____ / 2
Pronunciation 1 . . . . _____ / 3
Pronunciation 2 . . . . _____ / 3
Reading . . . . _____ / 4

</td></tr>
</table>

B.2 Bad News

As you complete each section of the CD-ROM course, make a check (✓). Write your scores for the Review Quiz.

<table>
<tr><td>

Video Listening
_____ **1.** Pre-listening
_____ **1.** Listening for Information
_____ **1.** Listening for Ideas
_____ **2.** Pre-listening
_____ **2.** Listening for Information
_____ **2.** Listening for Ideas

Vocabulary
_____ Phrases with *Feel*
_____ Practice

Speaking
_____ Language Functions: Talking about Possibilities
_____ Language Functions: Practice
_____ Role Play 1
_____ Role Play 2

Grammar
_____ **1.** Gerunds as Subjects and Objects
_____ **2.** Modals of Possibility
_____ **3.** Reflexive Pronouns

Task Listening
_____ Privacy

</td><td>

Pronunciation
_____ **1.** Loss of the *h* Sound in Pronouns
_____ **2.** The Vowel Sounds in *stop* and *just*

Reading
_____ Pre-reading
_____ Preview vocabulary
_____ Building a News Story
_____ Comprehension Check

Review Quiz   **Score**
Listening for information . . . . _____ / 7
Listening for ideas . . . . _____ / 3
Vocabulary . . . . _____ / 4
Speaking . . . . _____ / 6
Grammar 1 . . . . _____ / 3
Grammar 2 . . . . _____ / 4
Grammar 3 . . . . _____ / 3
Pronunciation 1 . . . . _____ / 3
Pronunciation 2 . . . . _____ / 3
Reading . . . . _____ / 4

</td></tr>
</table>

Name _____ Date _____

PROGRESS CHECKS

B.3 An Endorsement Deal

As you complete each section of the CD-ROM course, make a check (✓). Write your scores for the Review Quiz.

Video Listening
_____ 1. Pre-listening
_____ 1. Listening for Information
_____ 1. Listening for Ideas
_____ 2. Pre-listening
_____ 2. Listening for Information
_____ 2. Listening for Ideas

Vocabulary
_____ Verbs and Nouns
_____ Practice

Speaking
_____ Language Functions: Keeping a Conversation
_____ Language Functions: Practice
_____ Role Play 1
_____ Role Play 2

Grammar
_____ 1. Past Continuous
_____ 2. Modals of Preference
_____ 3. Comparative Adjectives

Task Listening
_____ Jingles

Pronunciation
_____ 1. The *er* Sound in *soccer*
_____ 2. The Voiceless *th* Sound in *think*

Reading
_____ Pre-reading
_____ Preview vocabulary
_____ Star Power
_____ Comprehension Check

Review Quiz   **Score**
Listening for information . . . . _____ / 7
Listening for ideas . . . . _____ / 3
Vocabulary . . . . _____ / 4
Speaking . . . . _____ / 6
Grammar 1 . . . . _____ / 4
Grammar 2 . . . . _____ / 3
Grammar 3 . . . . _____ / 3
Pronunciation 1 . . . . _____ / 3
Pronunciation 2 . . . . _____ / 3
Reading . . . . _____ / 4

B.4 No One by That Name

As you complete each section of the CD-ROM course, make a check (✓). Write your scores for the Review Quiz.

Video Listening
_____ 1. Pre-listening
_____ 1. Listening for Information
_____ 1. Listening for Ideas
_____ 2. Pre-listening
_____ 2. Listening for Information
_____ 2. Listening for Ideas

Vocabulary
_____ Are You Going to Yell?
_____ Practice

Speaking
_____ Language Functions: Expressing Certainty and Uncertainty
_____ Language Functions: Practice
_____ Role Play 1
_____ Role Play 2

Grammar
_____ 1. *Used to*
_____ 2. Embedded *Wh-* Questions
_____ 3. Indefinite Pronouns

Task Listening
_____ At the Reception Desk

Pronunciation
_____ 1. Unstressed Words (*of, at, for,* and *to*)
_____ 2. Reduced Phrases (*used to*)

Reading
_____ Pre-reading
_____ Preview vocabulary
_____ Anger Management
_____ Comprehension Check

Review Quiz   **Score**
Listening for information . . . . _____ / 7
Listening for ideas . . . . _____ / 3
Vocabulary . . . . _____ / 4
Speaking . . . . _____ / 6
Grammar 1 . . . . _____ / 3
Grammar 2 . . . . _____ / 4
Grammar 3 . . . . _____ / 3
Pronunciation 1 . . . . _____ / 3
Pronunciation 2 . . . . _____ / 3
Reading . . . . _____ / 4

PROGRESS CHECKS

C.1 No Help for Nick

As you complete each section of the CD-ROM course, make a check (✓). Write your
scores for the Review Quiz.

Video Listening
_____ **1.** Pre-listening
_____ **1.** Listening for Information
_____ **1.** Listening for Ideas
_____ **2.** Pre-listening
_____ **2.** Listening for Information
_____ **2.** Listening for Ideas

Vocabulary
_____ Cheer Up!
_____ Practice

Speaking
_____ Language Functions: Asking Permission and Offering Help
_____ Language Functions: Practice
_____ Role Play 1
_____ Role Play 2

Grammar
_____ **1.** Past Continuous with *when*
_____ **2.** Modals of Permission
_____ **3.** Comparisons with *as* + adjective + *as*

Task Listening
_____ Fashion Show

Pronunciation
_____ **1.** Unstressed Words (*as*)
_____ **2.** Linking Words Together

Reading
_____ Pre-reading
_____ Preview vocabulary
_____ Identity Theft
_____ Comprehension Check

Review Quiz	Score
Listening for information	_____ / 7
Listening for ideas	_____ / 3
Vocabulary	_____ / 4
Speaking	_____ / 6
Grammar 1	_____ / 4
Grammar 2	_____ / 4
Grammar 3	_____ / 2
Pronunciation 1	_____ / 3
Pronunciation 2	_____ / 3
Reading	_____ / 4

C.2 In the News

As you complete each section of the CD-ROM course, make a check (✓). Write your
scores for the Review Quiz.

Video Listening
_____ **1.** Pre-listening
_____ **1.** Listening for Information
_____ **1.** Listening for Ideas
_____ **2.** Pre-listening
_____ **2.** Listening for Information
_____ **2.** Listening for Ideas

Vocabulary
_____ Phrasal Verbs (Inseparable)
_____ Practice

Speaking
_____ Language Functions: Giving Opinions
_____ Language Functions: Practice
_____ Role Play 1
_____ Role Play 2

Grammar
_____ **1.** Inseparable Phrasal Verbs
_____ **2.** Gerunds and Infinitives
_____ **3.** Future Time Clauses

Task Listening
_____ Healthy Pleasures

Pronunciation
_____ **1.** Stress in Phrasal Verbs
_____ **2.** Reduced Phrases (*going to*)

Reading
_____ Pre-reading
_____ Preview vocabulary
_____ What's in a Name?
_____ Comprehension Check

Review Quiz	Score
Listening for information	_____ / 7
Listening for ideas	_____ / 3
Vocabulary	_____ / 4
Speaking	_____ / 6
Grammar 1	_____ / 3
Grammar 2	_____ / 4
Grammar 3	_____ / 3
Pronunciation 1	_____ / 3
Pronunciation 2	_____ / 3
Reading	_____ / 4

Name _____ Date _____

PROGRESS CHECKS

C.3 The Truth Revealed

As you complete each section of the CD-ROM course, make a check (✓). Write your scores for the Review Quiz.

Video Listening
_____ **1.** Pre-listening
_____ **1.** Listening for Information
_____ **1.** Listening for Ideas
_____ **2.** Pre-listening
_____ **2.** Listening for Information
_____ **2.** Listening for Ideas

Vocabulary
_____ They Wanted Me Out of the Way
_____ Practice

Speaking
_____ Language Functions: Expressing Necessity
_____ Language Functions: Practice
_____ Role Play 1
_____ Role Play 2

Grammar
_____ **1.** Infinitives of Purpose
_____ **2.** Modals of Necessity
_____ **3.** Participial Adjectives

Task Listening
_____ A New Contract

Pronunciation
_____ **1.** Reduced Phrases (*have to, want to, got to*)
_____ **2.** Pronunciation of *-ed* Endings

Reading
_____ Pre-reading
_____ Preview vocabulary
_____ Let's Make a Deal!
_____ Comprehension Check

Review Quiz	**Score**
Listening for information	_____ / 7
Listening for ideas	_____ / 3
Vocabulary	_____ / 4
Speaking	_____ / 6
Grammar 1	_____ / 4
Grammar 2	_____ / 3
Grammar 3	_____ / 3
Pronunciation 1	_____ / 3
Pronunciation 2	_____ / 3
Reading	_____ / 4

C.4 Dean's Challenge

As you complete each section of the CD-ROM course, make a check (✓). Write your scores for the Review Quiz.

Video Listening
_____ **1.** Pre-listening
_____ **1.** Listening for Information
_____ **1.** Listening for Ideas
_____ **2.** Pre-listening
_____ **2.** Listening for Information
_____ **2.** Listening for Ideas

Vocabulary
_____ Phrasal Verbs (Separable)
_____ Practice

Speaking
_____ Language Functions: Clarifying
_____ Language Functions: Practice
_____ Role Play 1
_____ Role Play 2

Grammar
_____ **1.** Present Perfect Continuous with *for* and *since*
_____ **2.** Separable Phrasal Verbs
_____ **3.** Superlative Adjectives

Task Listening
_____ Coaching Seminar

Pronunciation
_____ **1.** Consonant Clusters
_____ **2.** Intonation Showing Surprise

Reading
_____ Pre-reading
_____ Preview vocabulary
_____ How to Tell Who's Telling the Truth
_____ Comprehension Check

Review Quiz	**Score**
Listening for information	_____ / 7
Listening for ideas	_____ / 3
Vocabulary	_____ / 4
Speaking	_____ / 6
Grammar 1	_____ / 4
Grammar 2	_____ / 4
Grammar 3	_____ / 2
Pronunciation 1	_____ / 3
Pronunciation 2	_____ / 3
Reading	_____ / 4

A.1 | Another Busy Day

Listening

🎧 **A. Listen to Track 1.** *Amy is talking with Talia at the* Newsline *office. Circle the phrases you hear.*

1. **(You're working)/ You work** too hard.

2. Maybe you **should / could** mention that to Tony?

3. I **have / had** to work late tonight.

4. I **don't care about / I'm not taking care of** my hair.

5. You **may / could** be right.

6. **What was / What's** the homework?

7. **That's / That was** easy enough to do.

8. I guess **I can / I'll** do it after work.

🎧 **B. Listen to Track 2.** *Amy and Talia continue talking at the office and Tony joins them. Complete the lines from the dialog.*

1. **Amy:** Why don't you _____take a break_____ tonight?

2. **Talia:** I'm too _____ to go.

3. **Tony:** What are you _____ on?

4. **Amy:** She's always working. She told me _____.

5. **Tony:** I have a _____ for you to work on.

6. **Tony:** I know you've been hoping for _____.

7. **Tony:** By the way, you _____ different.

🎧 **C. Listen to Track 3.** *A journalism professor is describing two kinds of questions. Complete Amy's notes.*

Classic questions	Probing questions
• __Who__ did it?	• __Who else__ knows this?
• _____ happened?	• _____ about this?
• _____ did it happen?	• _____ did _____ about this?
• _____ was it?	• _____ your information?
• _____ did it happen?	• _____ about this?

Vocabulary

See Appendix 2 to review the vocabulary terms.

Talia is describing some people she met recently. Read the conversations and choose the adjective that best describes each person. Answer the questions with complete sentences.

cheerful	confident	depressed	energetic
serious	laid-back	nervous	relaxed

1. **Amy:** What do you think of Jake? I think he really likes you.

   Talia: Jake? Well, he smiles too much and he always acts so . . . happy.

   Amy: Smiles too much?! Always happy?! You know, most people *like* that, Talia!

   Talia: Well, I'm not "most people." He just doesn't understand me when I'm in a bad mood.

Talia   **Amy**

   How would you describe Jake?   He's cheerful. / He's too cheerful for Talia.

   Describe Jake using an opposite *word* + not.   He isn't depressed. / He's not serious enough for Talia.

2. **Amy:** How about Tom? He's great, isn't he?

   Talia: Tom? Well, he's nice, but he doesn't seem very sure of himself. And he seems kind of sad all the time.

   How would you describe Tom? _____

   Describe Tom using an opposite *word* + not. _____

3. **Amy:** And Richard? I suppose he's too good-looking and successful for you?

   Talia: No, not at all. But he's constantly moving—he never slows down for a moment. I'm exhausted just trying to keep up with him!

   How would you describe Richard? _____

   Describe Richard using an opposite *word* + not. _____

4. **Amy:** Well, how about Marcos? He's very calm and cool.

   Talia: Well, yeah. But he's so laid-back that it just drives me crazy!

   How would you describe Marcos? _____

   What's another way you could say the same thing? _____

5. **Amy:** OK, Talia. I know for a fact you like Luke.

    Talia: Yes, but it's always a problem when people work too hard. They get nervous and anxious, and it's difficult to be around them.

    Amy: Is that what you think of Luke?

    Talia: No. . . . That's what *he* thinks of *me*!

    How does Luke describe Talia? _____

    What's another way you could say the same thing? _____

Grammar 1

Simple Present and Present Continuous*

Complete the conversations. Circle the correct verb tense.

1. **Amy:** Hey, Talia. I **talk /(ʼm talking)** to Josh right now on the phone. He **wants / ʼs wanting** to know if you're coming to the party.

    Talia: Oh, could you give me the phone, please? Hello, Josh. Hi. . . . Listen. I **work /**

    ʼm working on an important project at the moment. I really can't make it to the party.

    Josh: OK, I **understand / am understanding**. But we'll miss you. You always **tell / are telling** great stories.

2. **Amy:** So **do you know / are you knowing** Steve Adams, the guy in the accounting department? I can introduce you.

    Talia: Amy! You always **want / are wanting** to introduce me to guys!! I **don't look / ʼm not**

    looking for a boyfriend right now.

    Amy: I **ʼm knowing / know** that. But just wait until you meet Steve. You'll change your mind!

3. **Amy:** What **do you two laugh / are you two laughing** about?

    Claire: Oh, nothing. Just Talia's hair.

    Amy: Poor Talia. She **works / ʼs working** too much these days. She just **doesn't have / isn't**

    having time to do her hair in the morning.

    Tina: Hey! That gives me a great idea for a report on lifestyles! Why don't we interview hair stylists about some easy hairstyles for working women? A lot of us **don't usually have /**

    aren't usually having much time in the mornings.

    Claire: That's a great idea! We **never do / ʼre never doing** stories like that! I'm sure our viewers will love it.

---

*To review the grammar points, see the Grammar Explanations at the end of each unit.

Grammar 2

Expressions for Suggesting

A. *Amy is giving some suggestions to people at* Newsline. *Correct the mistakes in each suggestion. If there's no error, write* OK *at the end of the line.*

1. If you have some questions about the article, why ~~do you not~~ *don't you* ask Tony?

2. How about to call our report on retirement "Let's Call It a Day?"

3. Let's taking a coffee break in a few minutes, OK?

4. I know Jake loves movies. Why don't invite him to come with us? Come on—let's ask him!

5. How about a quick snack before we get back to work?

6. If you're tired, why not you leave work a little early today? You work too hard!

B. *Now write some suggestions for people you know.*

EXAMPLE: **(You and your classmate)** Why don't we study together tonight?

1. **(Your English teacher)** _____

2. **(Your friend)** _____

3. **(You and a friend)** _____

Grammar 3

Infinitives with *Too* and *Enough*

A. *Make sentences with* too *and* enough. *There is 1 extra word in each group.*

1. Talia / works / to become a reporter some day / enough / too / hard

    Talia works hard enough to become a reporter some day.

2. Amy / writes / too / enough / well / to pass her journalism class

    _____

3. Amy / is / nice / too / enough / to help Talia

    _____

4. Tony / to talk with Talia now / enough / too / is / busy

_____

5. John Connelly / listens / carefully / enough / too / to do great interviews

_____

6. There / enough / time / to take a break / isn't / too / for Talia

_____

B. Now write some sentences about yourself with too *and* enough. *Think about your schedule, your budget, your job or school.*

EXAMPLES: **(too)**   I have too much homework tonight to go out with my friends.

         (enough)   I don't have enough money to go out with my friends tonight.

1. _____

2. _____

3. _____

Language Functions

See Appendix 3 to review the language function charts.

A. Complete the conversation with the best expressions for giving, accepting, or declining invitations.

Jake: Hey, Talia, do (1)_____you want to_____ see a movie Friday night?

Talia: Well, I (2)_____, but I (3)_____ late on my report.
Maybe (4)_____.

Jake: Too bad. (5)_____ Saturday? Are you (6)_____ then?

Talia: Sorry, I (7)_____. I'm pretty busy all day. I'm
(8)_____ a friend with some decorating stuff, and then I have to
(9)_____ my course homework.

Jake: Gosh, you're so busy all the time! So (10)_____ go Sunday!

Talia: Sunday? Gee. I (11)_____ lunch with my parents.

Jake: Sunday night then? There's a show at 8:00. You can't say no!

Talia: Oh . . . OK. (12)_____. That (13)_____ great.
What's the movie?

B. *Complete the invitations. Note: 2 invitations are formal, and 2 are informal.*

1. **Your co-workers** (*invite, formal*): _____ on Saturday?

   You (*decline, formal*): Thank you, but I can't. Unfortunately, I

   _____ this weekend.

2. **Your friend** (*invite, informal*): How about a game of racquetball tonight?

   You (*decline, informal*): _____

3. **Your boss** (*invite, formal*): _____ lunch with us?

   You (*accept, formal*): _____

4. **Your boyfriend / girlfriend** (*invite, informal*): _____

   You (*accept, informal*): _____

Application Activities

> **Study Tip**
> Choose 2 or 3 Application Activities. Complete the activities this week!

1. **Grammar.** We can use the present or present continuous to make complaints with *always*; for example, *My roommate always forgets to clean the kitchen!* or *My roommate is always forgetting to clean the kitchen!* Think of some complaints about the people in your life (for example, your husband/wife, boyfriend/girlfriend, friend, roommate, boss, or people you see on the bus or train). Write 5 sentences making complaints with *always*.

2. **Vocabulary.** Review the vocabulary words in this unit about feelings. Think of 10 more words you know (or find 3 in a dictionary) that describe how people feel. Make vocabulary cards for the words. Write a sentence on each card using a new word.

3. **Writing.** Write 5 sentences about a "workaholic" you know. Who is this person? What kind of work does he or she do? Why do you think this person is a workaholic?

4. **Interview.** Interview a person about an important recent event (for example, an earthquake, a political election, a crime). Ask classic questions (*who, what, when, where*, etc.) and probing questions (*What do you think about this?* etc.). Report your findings to a classmate or to the whole class or write a short report about what you learned.

5. **Project.** Find out about how people spend their leisure time. Ask questions like this: *Is it more important to work very, very hard so that you can succeed in school/work? Is it more important to have a balanced life by not studying or working too hard?* Prepare a short report about people's attitudes about work and leisure time. Present your report to the class.

Grammar Explanations

This section contains the same grammar explanations that are found on the CD-ROM. They are included here for your quick reference. To view the animated presentation, go to the Grammar section of Unit A.1 in the CD-ROM course.

Grammar 1: Simple Present and Present Continuous

1. We use the **simple present** to talk about something that happens every day or all the time.
   Talia **works** hard.

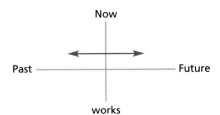

2. We use the **present continuous** to talk about something that is happening right now.
   She's **working** on a transportation story.

   We can also use the **present continuous** to talk about something that is happening these days—even if it is not happening right now.
   Talia **is working** hard **these days**.
   She's **taking** a journalism class **this semester**.

   Remember, when we speak, we almost always use contractions with pronouns and *be* and with nouns and *be*.
   She's talking.
   They're talking.
   Talia's talking.

3. We often use the **simple present** with **adverbs of frequency**, such as *always, usually, often, sometimes, rarely,* and *never.*

   If the main verb is a form of *be*, the adverb of frequency goes *after* the verb.
   Talia **is** at her desk before 8:00.
   Talia **is always** at her desk before 8:00.

   With all other verbs, adverbs of frequency go *before* the verb.
   I **work** hard.
   I **always work** hard.

4. We usually use *always* with the simple present. But when we complain about something, we may use *always* with the **present continuous**.
   Amy: She's **always working**. She has no time for fun.

5. Some verbs don't express actions. Verbs such as *want, like, know,* and *own* express feelings, thoughts, and possessions. They are called *non-action* (stative) verbs. We usually do not use non-action verbs in the present continuous. We're going to learn more about non-action verbs in Unit B.1.
   Tony **likes** Talia's work.
   We do **NOT** say: ~~Tony is liking Talia's work.~~

Grammar 2: Expressions for Suggesting

1. We often use **let's** + the **base form** of the verb to make a suggestion.
   Let's go home.

   Let's is short for *Let us*. But we always use *let's*.
   It means: Here's a suggestion for you and me.

2. Another way to make a suggestion is with **Why don't** + a **subject** + the **base form** of the verb.
   Why don't you **go** to the party with me tonight?

   You can use different subjects with this expression.
   Ana's car isn't working? **Why doesn't she** come with us?
   That's a good idea. I'll call her.

   When you make a suggestion with **Why don't**, you are asking a question. If you are writing, remember to use a question mark.
   Why don't we meet at 9:00?

3. Another expression we use for suggestions is **How about**. After *How about*, you can use a verb + *-ing* or a noun.
   How about going to a movie tonight?
   How about a movie tonight?

   Expressions with *How about* are also questions. Don't forget the question mark in your writing!

4. You can also use **Why not** + the **base form** of the verb to make a suggestion. We usually don't begin a conversation with *Why not*. We use it as a response.
   Meg: I don't feel like staying home tonight.
   Brian: **Why not come** with us to Josh's party?

   Notice that with *Why not* we don't use the subject.

   We do **NOT** say: ~~Why not you come with us to Josh's party?~~

   Expressions with *Why not* are questions. Don't forget the question mark in your writing!

Grammar 3: Infinitives with *Too* and *Enough*

1. We often use *too* with an **adjective + the infinitive** when we explain why something is impossible.

   Amy: Josh is having a party tonight. Do you want to go?

   Talia: I can't go. I'm **too tired to go**.

   In the conversation, Talia means she's very tired and that's the reason she can't go. *Tired* is an adjective. *To go* is the infinitive.

   I'm tired.

   I'm **too tired to go**.

2. We can also use *too* with an **adverb + the infinitive**.

   Amy: Did you watch *Newsline* last night?

   Will: No, I got home **too late to see** it.

   In the example, *late* is an adverb and *to see* is the infinitive.

3. We can use *enough* with an **adjective (or an adverb) + the infinitive** when we explain why something is possible. Notice that *enough* goes after the adjective or adverb.

   Amy: For homework, we have to compare two news stories on the same topic.

   Talia: That's **easy enough to do**. I can do that.

   Talia means that the assignment is easy, and that's the reason she can do it.

   That's easy.

   That's **easy enough to do**.

4. Notice the **difference in word order** when we use *too* or *enough*. **Too** goes **before** the adjective or adverb.

   It's **too hard** to understand.

   Enough goes **after** the adjective or adverb.

   It's **easy enough** to understand.

5. We can also add ***for*** + a **noun or pronoun** before the infinitive.

   Talia: Can you get me that folder on top of the bookcase?

   Amy: Sure. It's easy enough **for me to reach**.

A.2 Breaking News

🎧 **A. Track 4.** *Tony is telling Talia and Amy about an audiocassette that the* Newsline *office received. Unscramble the sentences. Then listen to Track 4 to check your answers.*

1. you heard player of Have Nick Crawford, the soccer ever

   Have you ever heard of Nick Crawford, the soccer player?

2. ago Apparently conversation took place This a while

   _____

3. into lately There's fallen rumor a debt that he's

   _____

4. gossip sorts I've heard of all that about

   _____

5. Also on $50,000 him a woman offers the tape

   _____

6. this Nick will tape If is real, be Crawford history

   _____

7. won't he play the match to get in next You mean,

   _____

🎧 **B. Listen to Track 5.** *Talia is talking with Tony about Nick Crawford. Complete the conversation.*

Tony: Is there a (1)_____?

Talia: Not (2)_____. I'll do it. It's just that . . . I know Nick Crawford.

Tony: You do?

Talia: Yes. We went to college together. It's (3)_____ to believe he would do something like this.

Tony: Well, (4)_____ and smell the (5)_____, Talia! He's a big star now. He's been a star on the national team for 4 years now. People do (6)_____ things when they get (7)_____.

Talia: I just can't believe it. Nick Crawford taking a bribe?

Tony: Listen, Talia. You're (8)_____. You're a (9)_____

researcher, and one day—I hope—you'll be a (10)_____ reporter.

But don't (11)_____ your (12)_____ get in the way of

your work. If you do, I'll have to find someone else to work on this story.

🎧 **C. Listen to Track 6.** *You will hear a short biography of Lance Armstrong, a professional cyclist. Answer the question based on the information that you hear.*

At one time, Lance Armstrong said, "I used to ride my bike to make a living. Now I just want to live so that I can ride." What do you think he means?

_____

_____

Vocabulary

See Appendix 2 to review the vocabulary terms.

Here are some authentic *names and items. Do you know them? Complete the conversations below about the items. Circle the correct adjective.*

Rolex® An expensive brand of watch	**Equal®** A popular sweetener used instead of sugar	**Luau** A popular type of Hawaiian party	**Spam®** A synthetic meat product	**Babe Ruth** A famous American baseball player	**cubic zirconium** A synthetic gem that looks like a diamond
Tiffany® A famous maker of glass art items	**Wedgwood®** A British maker of china (porcelain dishes)	**Rembrandt** A famous seventeenth-century Dutch painter	**Chanel®** A famous maker of French perfumes	**EBay®** An auction site on the Internet where people can sell items	

1. **Sarah:** I love your perfume! Is it Chanel?

   Amy: No. I couldn't afford Chanel, so I bought a **fake / sincere**

   perfume. It smells the same as the real thing, but it's not so

   expensive.

2. **Tony:** Amy, Talia. I have a story for you to work on. It seems that

   the local museum has purchased a **bogus / dishonest**

   Rembrandt from a **crooked / fake** dealer.

   Amy: You're kidding!

   Tony: I'm afraid it's true. I want you two to do an article on how to

   recognize a(n) **artificial / trustworthy** art dealer.

Rembrandt's *The Night Watch* (1642)

3. **Josh:** How was your trip to Hawaii?

 Tom: Fantastic. The last night we were there, we went to a luau.

 Josh: A real luau?

 Tom: Actually, it wasn't very **sincere / authentic**—the dancers weren't real Hawaiians, and we ate Spam instead of roast pig, but it was a lot of fun.

4. **Amy:** I have some great gossip to tell you! I heard a rumor that Jeremy bought a cubic zirconium for his fiancée's wedding ring!

 Talia: No! You're joking! And Jenna still doesn't know it's not an **actual / honest** diamond?

 Amy: Nope. She thinks it's a **real / correct** diamond.

 Talia: Wow, that Jeremy sounds like a(n) **honest / dishonest** guy to me!

5. **Claire:** I finally took my great-grandmother's old china and lamps into an antique store to find out how much they're worth.

 Todd: What did you find out?

 Claire: Well, it turns out that the china is **authentic / phony** Wedgwood, so it's worth a lot. And the lamps are by Tiffany, so they're pretty **valuable / worthless**, too.

6. **Talia:** Is this guy **artificial / for real**? He's trying to sell me a Rolex watch for 20 bucks.

 Amy: You'd better not buy it. It's either a **fake / genuine** or it's stolen!

7. **Tina:** Thanks for the tea. Do you have any Equal?

 Leanne: Sorry. Just sugar. I can't stand **phony / artificial** sweeteners.

8. **Tony:** I bought this baseball for my son. A guy on an Internet auction site told me it was signed by Babe Ruth.

 John: I hate to tell you this, Tony, but this is a **phony / crooked** signature. I'm a big collector, and I can tell you this signature is not real.

Babe Ruth

Grammar 1

Present Perfect for Indefinite Past

Tony is talking to a new reporter about the news business. Complete the conversations. Use the present perfect to describe the indefinite past.

1. **Allison:** How long (**you / work**) _____have you worked_____ for *Newsline*?

   Tony: (**I / be**) _____ here for a long, long time.

2. **Allison:** Well, how long (*Newsline* / **be in business**) _____?

   Tony: Since 1975. We (**build**) _____ a great reputation in television news.

3. **Allison:** Does *Newsline* have plans to expand its news business?

   Tony: Oh, sure. We (**recently / start**) _____ Internet broadcasts. We'll expand even more next year.

4. **Allison:** (**you / ever do**) _____ a really difficult interview?

   Tony: Oh, gosh. (**I / report**) _____ hundreds of difficult interviews and stories.

5. **Allison:** What (**you / learn**) _____ the news business?

   Tony: (**I / have**) _____ a lot of good teachers. (**lately / I / learn**) _____ not to talk so much.

Grammar 2

Modals of Advice

A. *Some people are giving advice. Rephrase the advice statements below. Use the words in parentheses.*

1. **Amy:** Don't work so hard! (**shouldn't**)

   You shouldn't work so hard.

2. **Tony:** You could ask Claire to help you with the story. (**ought to**)

   _____

3. **Tony:** It's important not to let your feelings get in the way of your work. (**Don't**)

   _____

4. **Tony:** Please make a copy of this tape in case something happens to it! (**had better**)

   _____

5. **Amy:** It would be a good idea to find out if the tape is authentic. (**ought to**)

   _____

B. *Respond to Talia by giving her some advice. Use* should, shouldn't, ought to, *or* had better.

1. **Talia:** I'm exhausted! I think this coffee is making me feel *more* tired, not *less* tired!!!

    <u>You shouldn't drink so much coffee.</u>

2. **Talia:** I'm afraid the audio department is going to close soon.

3. **Talia:** I haven't had a thing to eat all day!

4. **Talia:** Last time I waited until the last minute to do my journalism assignment. I want to do a better job this time.

5. **Talia:** I think Amy will be mad at me for not going to the party.

Study Tip
Review the Grammar Explanations. Highlight 3 explanations. Write another example for each one.

Grammar 3

Future with *Will* and *Be going to*

A. *Choose the best response to complete each conversation.*

  <u> d </u> **1.** There's a U2 concert at the Paladium tonight.

  <u>   </u> **2.** Did Anita come to work today?

  <u>   </u> **3.** Did you hear? Bailey is injured. He won't play in the final game.

  <u>   </u> **4.** Hey, Tommy. Get down off that table. You're going to fall.

  <u>   </u> **5.** Why is Talia going to see Phil now?

  <u>   </u> **6.** Hey, Josh. The phone is ringing.

a. I'm not sure. I'll go and find out.

b. No, I'm not. I'll be OK.

c. She's going to give him a tape.

d. I think I'll go. Do you want to go, too?

e. I'll get it.

f. Oh, no! That's too bad. Then the Giants will probably lose.

B. *Write some sentences about yourself in the future.*

EXAMPLE: <u>This weekend I'm going to go to a birthday party.</u>

1. **(this weekend)**

2. **(next year)**

3. **(in 5 years)**

Language Functions

See Appendix 3 to review the language function charts.

A. *Read the conversations. Correct the mistakes in the boldfaced phrases. If the phrase is correct, write* OK.

there's a rumor that

1. **Amy:** Hey, Talia, ~~they say a rumor that~~ you're going to get a big story to cover.

   Talia: **No way! You're incredible!** What story?

2. **Amy:** Tony, **have you listened to this**? Someone tried to shoot the president!

   Tony: You're serious! That's incredible! What happened?

3. **Talia: Guess that! I am hearing** our journalism professor has been fired!

   Amy: Way! I don't believe! I thought he was great.

4. **Tony: Hear this! They tell** that 10 years from now, 50 percent of college degrees will be done through the Internet.

   Amy: You're kidding! Not a way! There's no substitute for a real live teacher in a classroom.

B. *Write a short dialog about a rumor or some "fake news." Possible topics are sports, entertainment, or politics.*

Tell someone news: _____

Respond to the news: _____

Application Activities

1. **Grammar.** Write a short report about a popular athlete in your country. Talk about his or her history and the reasons he or she is popular. Use the present perfect for past events at an indefinite time in the past.

2. **Vocabulary.** Make a "word web." Write the word *authentic* in the middle of the web. Expand your web with types of authentic things (for example, types of clothing). Write the brand names or people that are associated with these things. Try to write at least 20 items in your word web.

3. **Writing.** Write a paragraph about a famous person who has been involved in a scandal. Find out different sides of the story.

4. **Speaking.** Think of at least 3 gossip newspapers, magazines, and television shows that talk about famous people and are popular in your country. Do you like them? Why or why not? Discuss with your classmates.

5. **Project.** Find out about the personal challenges of any of these famous actors and models: Christopher Reeve, Heather Mills McCartney, Oprah Winfrey, Waris Dirie, Michael J. Fox, or Marilyn Monroe. If you wish to use the Internet, use a search engine such as Google and type in the name of the person. Tell your classmates about what you learned or write a short report.

Grammar Explanations

This section contains the same grammar explanations that are found on the CD-ROM. They are included here for your quick reference. To view the animated presentation, go to the Grammar section of Unit A.2 in the CD-ROM course.

Grammar 1: Present Perfect for Indefinite Past

1. We use the **present perfect** to talk about something that happened at some time in the past (but not at any particular time). We call this the **indefinite past**. *Indefinite* means that we don't give an exact time. The time of the event is not important, or we don't know it.
   Talia: Have you **listened** to the tape?
   Tony: Yes, John and I **have** both **listened** to it.

   Talia isn't interested in **when** Tony listened to the tape. She wants to know only if he has heard the tape so that he can tell her about it.

   We do **NOT** say: ~~They have listened to the tape yesterday.~~

The Present Perfect
I **have been** there.
You **have been** there.
He/She/It **has been** there.
We **have been** there.
They **have been** there.

2. We often use *ever* in questions about the indefinite past. It means "at some time before now."
   Tony: Have you **ever heard** of Nick Crawford?
   Talia: Yes, I have.

   Notice that the word *ever* goes before the past participle *heard*.
   Have you **ever** heard of Nick Crawford?

3. We often use *never* with the present perfect. It means "at no time before now."

   Never also goes before the past participle.
   Amy: My sister **has never heard** of Nick Crawford.
   Talia: Has she ever been to a soccer game?
   Amy: No, never. And she's **never watched** one on TV.

4. We can use the present perfect with *just, recently,* and *lately* to talk about things that happened in the very recent past.

   In American English it is more common to use the simple past tense with *just*. We also sometimes use the simple past with *recently*. The meaning is the same.
   Tony **has just received** a tape.
   OR
   Tony **just received** a tape.

   Someone **has recently offered** Nick money.
   OR
   Someone **recently offered** Nick money.

With the present perfect, *just* comes before the past participle. *Recently* often comes at the end of the sentence.
   Someone **has offered** Nick money **recently**.

Lately has a similar meaning to *recently*, but we only use it with the present perfect. We do not use it with the simple past, and we do not use it for a one-time event. Notice that *lately* does not go before the past participle. It usually goes at the end of the sentence.
   He's **fallen** into debt **lately**.
   We do **NOT** say: ~~He fell into debt lately.~~

Grammar 2: Modals of Advice

1. We use ***should*** and ***ought to*** to give advice.
   You **should take** a break.
   You **ought to take** a break.

2. We use ***should*** to ask for advice. We don't use *ought to* in questions.
   Should I **take** a journalism class?

3. The negative of *should* is ***shouldn't***. We don't use the negative of *ought to* in American English.
   We **shouldn't give away** our only copy of the tape.

4. We can also use ***had better*** to give **advice**. *Had better* is stronger than *should* or *ought to*. We use it when we think that something bad will happen if the person does not follow the advice.
   We'd **better find out** fast, or we'll lose the story.

   We'd better is the contraction for *we had better*. We almost always use the contraction.
   we'd better
   you'd better

   The negative of *had better* is ***had better not***.
   We'd **better not be** late.

   We don't ask questions with *had better*.

5. Notice that *should, ought to,* and *had better* are followed by the **base form** of the verb.
   You **should take** a break.
   You **ought to take** a break.
   You'd **better take** a break.

6. When we give advice, we often use ***maybe*** or ***I think*** to be more polite.
   Maybe you should take a break.

Grammar 3: Future with *Will* and *Be Going to*

1. We can use **will** or its contraction (*'ll*) to talk about **future plans**.
   Amy: Is the tape real?
   Talia: We'll **find out**. I'll **get** this tape to an expert.

2. We also use **will** to make **predictions** (things that we think will happen).
   Tony: We'll probably **lose** the next match.

3. We use **will** for all subjects. It is followed by the base form of the verb.
   I'll lose.
   You'll lose.
   He'll lose.
   She'll lose.
   It'll lose.
   We'll lose.
   They'll lose.

4. The **negative** for *will* is **will not**. The contraction is **won't**. We usually use the contraction.
   We will not win without Nick.
   We **won't win** without Nick.

5. We can also use **be going to** to talk about **future plans** or to make **predictions**. It is followed by the base form of the verb.
   Amy: Is the tape real?
   Talia: We're **going to find out**. I'm going to **call** the audio department. They're probably **going to need** some time to analyze the tape.

   I'm going to call.
   You're going to call.
   He's going to call.
   She's going to call.
   It's going to call.
   We're going to call.
   They're going to call.

6. We use **be going to**, not **will**, when something in the present causes us to make a prediction.
   Amy: Look at those 2 players! They're **going to fall**.

   We do **NOT** say: ~~They'll fall~~.

   Talia is reaching for the phone. She's **going to call** the audio department.

   We do **NOT** say: ~~She'll call the audio department~~.

7. We use **will**, not **be going to**, when we decide to do something at the moment of speaking.
   John: There's a football game on TV tonight.
   Anne: Really? I think I'll **watch** it.

   We also use **will** to make an **offer**.
   Anne: Someone's at the door.
   John: I'll **see** who it is.

   We use **will** to make **promises**, too.
   Tony: Tell the audio department we need someone fast.
   Talia: Don't worry. I'll **tell** them.

A.3 A Job for Talia

🎧 **A. Listen to Track 7.** *Talia is listening to the tape. Tony is talking with her. Who or whose does each underlined word refer to?*

1. We'll pay <u>you</u> $50,000. ___Nick___

2. Do that, and $50,000 is <u>yours</u>. ___Nick's___

3. When will <u>we</u> have the results? _____ and _____

4. <u>He's</u> going to call me back this afternoon. _____

5. What do <u>you</u> mean? _____

6. Why would he do something to hurt <u>his</u> career? _____

7. Is he a friend of <u>yours</u>? _____

8. <u>We</u> had English together for 2 semesters. _____ and _____

🎧 **B. Listen to Track 8.** *Tony and Talia are talking about Talia's job. Complete this part of the conversation. Use the words in the box.*

big	break	chance	day	sorry	story	what	yours

1. **Talia:** Give me a ___chance___. What do you have to lose?

2. **Tony:** I'll give you 1 more _____.

3. **Talia:** You won't be _____.

4. **Tony:** You deserve a _____.

5. **Tony:** I'll tell you _____: Come up with something _____ and the story is _____.

6. **Tony:** Don't let him charm you out of a _____.

🎧 **C. Listen to Track 9.** *You will hear 3 phone messages. Claire needs to tell Talia, Tony, and Amy their messages. Complete the sentences.*

1. **Talia:** Did anyone call me?

   Claire: Yes, ___Bill Brown___ from _____ called you. He said that he has _____ you requested. He wants you to _____ before tomorrow _____. His number is _____, extension _____.

2. Tony: Anybody call while I was out?

    Claire: Yes, _____ from _____ in _____. He

        said that he has some _____ about a story. He said to call him on his

        _____, between _____ and _____ today.

3. Amy: Were there any calls for me?

    Claire: Yes, you got a call from _____. He said that he lost

        _____. He also wants to know if _____. He said you

    can call him back at _____.

Vocabulary

See Appendix 2 to review the vocabulary terms.

Read parts of an interview with Nick Crawford's parents. Choose the correct vocabulary word from the box. You won't use all of the words. Be careful to choose the correct form (noun or adjective).

Noun	Adjective	Noun	Adjective
business	businesslike	competition	competitive
emotion	emotional	injury	injured
professional	professional	confident	confidence
innocence	innocent	nation	national
pleasure	pleasant	shame	shameful
truth	truthful	surprise	surprised / surprising

Interviewer: How do you feel about all the attention Nick has received?

Mary Crawford: This is just such an (1) emotional_____ experience for us. It's hard to believe Nick

    is playing against the best players in the (2) nation_____!

Interviewer: You sound (3) s_____. Didn't you think Nick would someday be a star

    soccer player?

Harold Crawford: To be honest, I knew he was good, but I never thought he would make it to the

    (4) n_____ team. It was truly a (5) p_____ surprise the day we

    found out he made the team.

Interviewer: What was Nick like as a child? Was he a good soccer player back then?

Mary: Nick was always (6) c_____ as a child. He liked to win. We put him

    on junior soccer teams, and he even entered several soccer (7) c_____ as

    a teenager.

Interviewer: When Nick went to college, what did he study?

Harold: Well, he always knew he wanted to be a (8) p_____ soccer player, but he

    majored in (9) b_____ so he would have another option.

Interviewer: Tell me, how do you feel about Nick's recent (10) i_____?

Harold: Well, it's really a (11) s_____ that Nick was (12) i_____ and had to sit out the last game, but I'm (13) c_____ he'll be back out there on that field in no time.

Grammar 1

Present Perfect and Simple Past

Complete the paragraphs about Tony and his wife, Elisa. Use the present perfect or past tense of the verbs in parentheses, for *or* since, *and numbers. Check the timeline to help you fill in dates.*

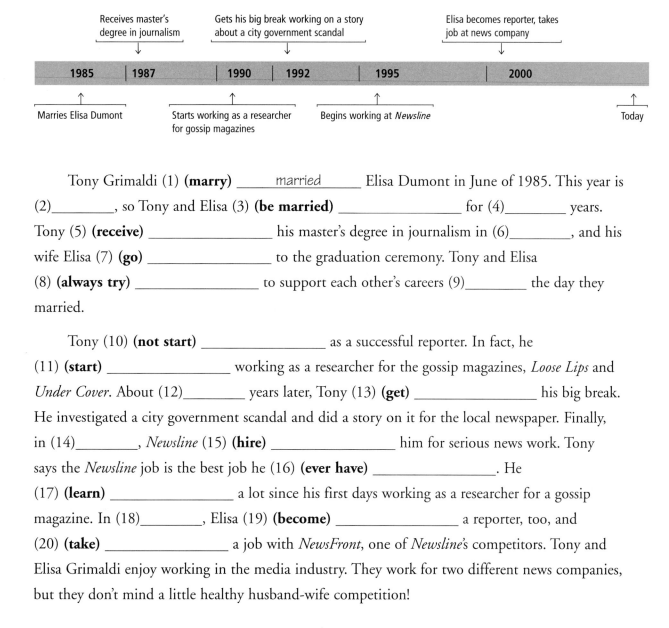

Tony Grimaldi (1) **(marry)** _____married_____ Elisa Dumont in June of 1985. This year is (2)_____, so Tony and Elisa (3) **(be married)** _____ for (4)_____ years. Tony (5) **(receive)** _____ his master's degree in journalism in (6)_____, and his wife Elisa (7) **(go)** _____ to the graduation ceremony. Tony and Elisa (8) **(always try)** _____ to support each other's careers (9)_____ the day they married.

Tony (10) **(not start)** _____ as a successful reporter. In fact, he (11) **(start)** _____ working as a researcher for the gossip magazines, *Loose Lips* and *Under Cover*. About (12)_____ years later, Tony (13) **(get)** _____ his big break. He investigated a city government scandal and did a story on it for the local newspaper. Finally, in (14)_____, *Newsline* (15) **(hire)** _____ him for serious news work. Tony says the *Newsline* job is the best job he (16) **(ever have)** _____. He (17) **(learn)** _____ a lot since his first days working as a researcher for a gossip magazine. In (18)_____, Elisa (19) **(become)** _____ a reporter, too, and (20) **(take)** _____ a job with *NewsFront*, one of *Newsline's* competitors. Tony and Elisa Grimaldi enjoy working in the media industry. They work for two different news companies, but they don't mind a little healthy husband-wife competition!

Grammar 2

Modals of Ability

KEY ORIGINALS

Amy has been interviewing successful people in her community for a story about "big breaks." Rewrite Amy's summary of this interview with Qi-Ping Li, a Chinese-American tailor, replacing the boldfaced phrases. Use a positive or negative modal of ability. Be sure to use the appropriate tense.

1. Qi-Ping Li **learned to sew** when he was 10.

   (sew) ___Qi-Ping Li could sew when he was 10.___

2. Qi-Ping's parents **didn't have enough money** to buy their children expensive clothes.

   (afford) ___Qi-Ping's parent weren't able to afford to buy their children expensive clothes.___

3. By the time he was a teenager, he **was creating** fashionable dresses and suits.

   (create) _____

4. Once when he was 16, he broke his clothing-making record: He **finished** 10 outfits in 1 day!

   (finish) _____

5. So many people started coming to his workshop that Qi-Ping **had trouble handling** all the orders.

   (handle) _____

6. Qi-Ping **borrowed** money from a bank and opened a small factory. That was his big break.

   (borrow) _____

7. Today, Qi-Ping and the employees of his company, Key Originals, **produce** 500 garments a day.

   (produce) _____

Grammar 3

Possessive Pronouns

Dean Bishop is a popular player on the national soccer team. Read about Dean's past. Complete the sentences on page 21. Use the words in the box.

he	him	his	Dean
Dean's	them	they	their
theirs	us	our	you
your	yours	yourself	me
my	mine		

What makes national soccer star Dean Bishop so successful? He just turned 30 years of age, and the world is (1)_____his_____. Everybody wants to see (2)_____. On a recent trip to Asia with the national team, Japanese and Korean fans fell in love with (3)_____. Young women especially love (4)_____. And both young men and women love to buy (5)_____ #8 soccer jerseys.

Fans of top British club Manchester United thought he was (6)_____ forever, until he moved to the United States in 2002. That was (7)_____ big break. Now Bishop is a member of the U.S. national team, sharing the spotlight with (8)_____ fellow star Nick Crawford.

Life isn't always as easy for (9)_____ idols as we think. Dean started at Manchester when he was 16, but (10)_____ didn't play a full game for 3 years. Once (11)_____ coach told him he was too short and too slow to play professional soccer. But Dean has refused to give up. (12)_____ spirit is too strong to quit!

In a recent interview with *Dash*, a reporter asked Dean, "What is (13)_____ most important goal right now?" Dean answered, "The national championship. That's all that matters to (14)_____."

Language Functions

See Appendix 3 to review the language function charts.

Complete the conversations. Use appropriate phrases for proposing an idea, hesitating, and convincing.

1. **Emilio** (*proposing an idea*): Say, Dad, can I _____ by you?

    Dad: OK. What is it?

    Emilio: Well, I know you're thinking of hiring a painter to paint the house?

    Dad: Yes . . .

    Emilio (*convincing*): Well, maybe I could paint the house, and you can pay me!
    _____. What do you think?

    Dad   (*responding, not yet convinced*): Hmmm. I'm _____ . . .

    Emilio (*convincing*): Oh, _____, Dad! _____. I know I can do it.

    Dad: (*responding, not yet convinced*) _____ . . . Well, all right, then. I'll give you a chance.

2. **Laila** (*proposing an idea*): Hey, Mom, _____ about something.

   Mom: You have? What is it?

   Laila: I'm thinking about taking a kick boxing class after school.

   Mom (*responding, not yet convinced*): Kick boxing? _____ . . .

   Laila (*convincing*): _____ . It'll be fun!

   Mom: All right. But you'll have to be careful.

BONUS
Write a dialog between you and your mother/father, your spouse/boyfriend/girlfriend, or your boss.
Propose a new idea and be convincing!

You (*proposing an idea*): _____

Your _____ (*responding, not yet convinced*): _____ .

You (*convincing*): _____

Your _____: _____ .

You: Thanks! I knew you'd understand!

Application Activities

Study Tip
Don't forget! Use the CD-ROM Progress Checks on pages xix–xxiv. Add notes: new expressions.

1. **Vocabulary.** Find the *noun* forms of these adjectives: *urgent, creative, difficult, bored.* Find the *adjective* forms of these nouns: *stress, risk, influence, talent.* What other adjective/noun pairs do you know? Make a list of at least 20 pairs.

2. **Writing.** Have you ever had "a big break"? It could be anything positive and important that has happened in your career or in your personal life. Write a paragraph about it.

3. **Speaking.** Talk about your abilities now, in the past, and in the future. What *can/can't* you do now? What *could/couldn't* you do as a child? What do you hope you *will be able to do* in the future?

4. **Project.** Go on the Internet to find out about the background of your favorite singer, actor, or athlete. How did this person prepare for his or her career? When did this person get his or her "big break"?

Grammar Explanations

This section contains the same grammar explanations that are found on the CD-ROM. They are included here for your quick reference. To view the animated presentation, go to the Grammar section of Unit A.3 in the CD-ROM course.

Grammar 1: Present Perfect and Simple Past

1. We use the **present perfect** to talk about something that started in the past and continues to the present.
   Talia **has been** a researcher **for 3 years**.
   This means that Talia started her job as a researcher 3 years ago and she is *still* a researcher.

   We use *for* to express the length of time.
   I've been here **for 5 hours**.

   We use *since* to say when something started.
   I've been here **since 8:00**.
   I've been here **since my boss arrived**.

2. We use the **simple past** to talk about something that happened in the past and is finished.
   Talia **was** in the same English class as Nick for 2 semesters.
   This means that Talia is not in the same class as Nick now. The class is finished.

   Now
   Past —— was —— Future

3. We can also use the **present perfect** to talk about something that happened in the indefinite past. We learned about this in Unit A.2.
   Talia **has investigated** other scandals.

   Remember, we do not use time expressions with the present perfect for the indefinite past.

   We do **NOT** say: ~~Talia has investigated other scandals last year.~~

4. We use the **simple past** to talk about something that happened at a specific time in the past.
   Nick **came** here from England about **10 years ago**.

   We often use **time expressions** with the simple past.
   The conversation **took place** **several months ago**.
   Talia **got** to the office **at 8:00**.
   Amy **went** to a party **last week**.

Grammar 2: Modals of Ability

1. We use *can* to talk about **present ability**. It is followed by the base form of the verb.
   The audio expert **can decide** if the tape is real.
   Talia **can't tell** if the tape is real. She's not an expert.

Can't is the contraction for *cannot*. We usually use the contraction.
   cannot → **can't**
We use *can* with all subjects.

> **I can** record the conversation.
> **You can** record the conversation.
> **He can** record the conversation.
> **She can** record the conversation.
> **It can** record the conversation.
> **We can** record the conversation.
> **They can** record the conversation.

2. We also use *be able to* to talk about **present ability**, but *can* is more common.
   The audio expert **is able to decide** if the tape is real.
   Talia **isn't able to tell** if the tape is real.

   Remember, the verb *be* changes form with different subjects. It is followed by the base form of the verb.

> **I'm** able to do it.
> **You're** able to do it.
> **He's/She's/It's** able to do it.
> **We're** able to do it.
> **They're** able to do it.

3. We use *could* to talk about **past ability**.
   Talia **could read** when she was just 4 years old.

4. We also use *was* or *were able to* to talk about **past ability**.
   Talia **was able to read** when she was just 4 years old.

   When we talk about a specific, one-time achievement in the past, we use *was* or *were able to*. We do not use *could*.
   Talia **was able to finish** Sunday's crossword puzzle in just an hour.

   We do **NOT** say: ~~She could finish Sunday's crossword puzzle in just an hour.~~

5. We can use *couldn't* or *wasn't* (or *weren't*) *able to* to talk about **past inability**—including specific, one-time events.
   Talia entered a crossword contest last year. But she **wasn't able to finish** the puzzle.
   She **couldn't figure** out one of the words.

6. For all other forms and tenses we use *be able to*, not *can* or *could*. We use it after *to* for the infinitive, with the present perfect, and with the future.
   Talia hopes **to be able to** give Tony an answer soon.

Our expert **hasn't been able to** solve the problem since this morning.
I hope he**'ll be able to** solve it by tomorrow.

Grammar 3: Possessive Pronouns

1. There are several ways to talk about **possession**. You already know that we can use possessive adjectives, such as *my* and *your*.

   Talia: This is **my** story.

   We can also use **possessive pronouns**, such as *mine* and *yours*.

   Talia: The story is **mine**.

Possessive adjective	Possessive pronoun
my	**mine**.
your	**yours**.
This is **her** story.	The story is **hers**.
its	
our	**ours**.
their	**theirs**.

   Notice that there is no **possessive pronoun** for *it*.

2. We use a possessive pronoun instead of a possessive adjective plus a noun.

   The story is **your story**.
   The story is **yours**.

   In this example *yours* means *your story*.

   Possessive pronouns are never followed by nouns.

   We do **NOT** say: ~~The story is yours story.~~

3. We often use **possessive pronouns** with *of* after a noun in expressions like *a friend of mine*.

   Talia is **a friend of mine**.
   Nick was **a classmate of hers**.

4. We use the same possessive pronoun for singular and for plural nouns. The form of the pronoun doesn't change.

   That report **is mine**.
   Those reports **are mine**.

   We do **NOT** say: ~~Those reports are mines.~~

5. Possessive pronouns can go at the beginning or end of a sentence.

   This isn't Amy's hat. It's my hat.
   Hers is new. **Mine** is old.
   Those aren't Amy's gloves.
   Hers are red. The blue ones are **mine**.

6. We often use possessive pronouns to answer questions starting with *Whose*.

   Amy: **Whose** job is this?
   Talia: It's **his**.

   Note that *whose* is not the same as *who's* (*who is*).

   We do **NOT** say: ~~Who's job is this?~~

A.4 | A Matter of Trust

Listening

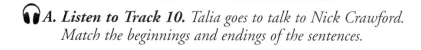

A. Listen to Track 10. *Talia goes to talk to Nick Crawford. Match the beginnings and endings of the sentences.*

___f___ **1.** I know you,

_____ **2.** After all these years,

_____ **3.** We were in an English literature class together,

_____ **4.** We studied together for the final,

_____ **5.** Are you a big

_____ **6.** I'm a researcher now

_____ **7.** I heard that there's a

a. I'm surprised you remember me.

b. soccer fan now?

c. didn't we?

d. nasty story coming out about me.

e. with *Newsline*.

f. don't I?

g. weren't we?

B. Listen to Track 11. *Talia is asking Nick to explain his side of the story. Fill in the blanks with an article or determiner (a, one, the, this). One blank has no article or determiner (∅).*

1. **Talia:** I want to hear your side of ___the___ story.

2. **Nick:** You're in _____ news business.

3. **Talia:** I told you _____ truth about why I was here, didn't I?

4. **Nick:** Look, the only goal I have right now is helping my team win _____ qualifying match next weekend.

5. **Nick:** After that, I will deal with _____ mess.

6. **Talia:** People say you threw _____ game. They think you have _____ gambling debts.

7. **Nick:** That's why I gave _____ Soccer Federation access to my bank accounts.

8. **Talia:** Did you or didn't you take _____ money?

9. **Talia:** The only story I want is _____ true story.

🎧 **C. Listen to Track 12.** *You will hear an announcement for a new TV program. Check (✓) the phrases that you hear.*

1.	✓	tune in this week	____	join us this week
2.	____	Each night this week is devoted only to	____	Each night this week is dedicated entirely to
3.	____	the master playwright and poet	____	the major writer and poet
4.	____	look at a lively time of Shakespeare	____	look at the life and times of Shakespeare
5.	____	we'll examine the fanciful comedies	____	we'll investigate principal comedies
6.	____	Shakespeare's historical plays	____	Shakespeare's stories and plays
7.	____	join us as we sample some of	____	join us as we send for some of
8.	____	with an in-depth exploration of	____	with an in-depth explanation of
9.	____	a selection from his 154 songs	____	a selection from his 154 sonnets
10.	____	your public service cable channel	____	your public serves a cable channel

Vocabulary

See Appendix 2 to review the vocabulary terms.

Josh and Amy are at their 10-year high school reunion. Complete their conversations. Fill in the blanks to create expressions with take.

1. Amy: Oh! __Take a look__ at the reunion schedule! The old cheerleading squad is planning a performance tonight! It's going to _____ in the hotel lobby at 10:00 p.m.

Josh: _____ from _____: They're not as good as they used to be!

Amy: How do you know?

Josh: I saw them practicing in the parking lot tonight. They were falling all over the place.

Amy: Well, in that case, let's _____ a _____ up front! It'll be fun to see!

2. Amy: Look at all the people. Who should we talk to first?

Josh: It doesn't matter. _____ your _____! I'm going to talk with the guys from the basketball team over there.

Amy: Uh-oh. There's one person I definitely *don't* want to talk to: Angie Taylor!

Josh: You didn't like her, did you?

> Washington High School 10 Year Reunion
> Tonight's Schedule

Amy: No! She stole my boyfriend!

Josh: Well, I don't want to _____. You know I can't choose between 2 old friends.

3. **Josh:** George Jacobsen! I haven't seen you in ages! What do you do now?

   George: I'm an insurance salesman. In fact, let me tell you about some great . . . !

   Josh: Uh, no, that's OK . . .

   George: Josh, you can trust me! _____ from _____ these great offers won't last long!

   Josh: No, thanks. I really don't need . . . . Oh, look! There's Amy Lee! Amy, Amy!

   George: Well, I'll tell you what. Here's a brochure. Think it over. _____ your _____. No hurry! Call me when you change your mind . . .

4. **Angie:** Great talking to you! _____, now. It sounds like your boss at *Newsline* is working you too hard!

   Amy: OK, I will. It was nice talking to you, too! _____!

   Josh: So, you and Angela are getting along now?

   Amy: Yeah, you know, time changes some people!

Grammar 1

Tag Questions

Complete the conversations. Fill in the correct tag questions.

1. **Jake:** Talia, you have brothers and sisters, _____don't you_____?

   Talia: I do. I have 1 brother and 1 sister.

2. **Amy:** You can join me after you finish work, _____?

   Talia: Sure. Wait, you're not trying to introduce me to another friend of yours, _____?

3. **Tony:** You weren't at the office all night last night, _____?

   Talia: No. I went home really late though—at midnight.

4. **Josh:** Talia is interested in me, _____?

   Amy: I won't say. You'll just have to find out for yourself, _____?

5. **Tony:** My wife called when I was out, _____?

   John: Yes, she left a message. I put it on your desk.

6. **Talia:** You couldn't help me with my class assignment, _____?

   Amy: I'm not the best person to ask. You know what my last grade was, _____?

Grammar 2

Study Tip
Try it out! Use new grammar points in your speech and writing. Keep track of which grammar points you use.

Adjectives and Adverbs

Amy and Josh went to the same high school. Now they're talking about their high school days. Read their comments about their former teachers. Fill in the blanks with the correct word. Add -ly if necessary. Sometimes more than 1 answer is possible.

loud	important	direct	cool	complete	angry
hard	patient	careful	boring	sweet	quick
easy	late	correct	bad	early	well
good	quiet				

1. Mrs. Carlton was really _____loud_____. You could hear her talking all the way down the hallway.

2. And remember Mr. Johanssen? He talked like a robot. His class was so _____ that I fell asleep almost every day!

3. When someone was _____, Mrs. Yamamoto would point at her watch and frown. It was really _____ to her to start class at 9 a.m. on the dot!

4. As soon as you got into Mrs. Yamamoto's class, you had to go _____ to your seat. She didn't like to see students standing around in her classroom.

5. Ms. Wright's class was really _____. You always had to check your paper _____ for typos and misspellings. If you didn't, she'd return your paper with a big red zero on it.

6. Mr. Tully didn't like it when students talked out of turn in his class. Once, I _____ asked a classmate if I could borrow a pencil. I just whispered! I hardly made any noise at all, but he yelled at me really _____.

7. Mr. Fong would let us leave _____ sometimes. And if you answered a question _____, he'd even throw you a piece of candy! He was so cool.

8. Mrs. Rodriguez was a really _____ math teacher. She answered all of your questions _____; she was never in a hurry. All her students loved her!

Articles

Complete the announcement about a new TV series. Fill in the correct articles (a, an, *or* the). *If no article is needed, write* ∅.

National TV, Channel 10, is going to broadcast (1)____a____ new series about (2)_____ life of William Shakespeare next week. (3)_____ series will be called *The Life and Times of Shakespeare*. On Monday, (4)_____ series will examine (5)_____ life of Shakespeare in (6)_____ England, from his birth in (7)_____ 1564 until his death in (8)_____ 1616.

On Tuesday, (9)_____ series will review (10)_____ comedies of Shakespeare, including *A Midsummer Night's Dream* and *The Comedy of Errors*. On Thursday, the series will feature (11)_____ tragedies of Shakespeare, including *Hamlet* and *Romeo and Juliet*. It's going to be (12)_____ very interesting series. You'll learn a lot about (13)_____ culture of England in (14)_____ 16th century. Be sure to tune in!

Language Functions

See Appendix 3 to review the language function charts.

A. Match the beginnings and ends of the expressions.

__f__	**1.** Excuse me, but haven't	**a.**	familiar, but I can't place you.
____	**2.** No, I'm sorry. You	**b.**	to see you again!
____	**3.** You look	**c.**	meeting you here!
____	**4.** Fancy	**d.**	met before.
____	**5.** I think we've	**e.**	must be mistaken.
____	**6.** I'm sorry . . .	**f.**	we met before?
____	**7.** It's great	**g.**	do I know you?

B. Josh recognizes someone at a supermarket. Complete the conversation, using an appropriate phrase from the language function charts.

Josh: Excuse me, (1)_____ Janet Jacobsen?

Janet: Yes, (2)_____. I'm (3)_____. Have we (4)_____?

Josh: Yes, remember? We (5)_____ at the Washington High School reunion last month. You're George's wife, right?

Jane: Oh, right! It's great to (6)_____.

Application Activities

1. **Grammar.** Look at a short newspaper or magazine story. Circle all phrases with *a* (or *an*). Underline all phrases with *the*. Which is more common—*a* or *the*? How many times is *a* (or *an*) used with "indefinite" nouns? How many times is *a* (or *an*) used with "first mention" nouns?

2. **Vocabulary.** Find 5 more English expressions that use *take*, such as *take someone seriously, take off*. There are lots of them! Share them with a classmate.

3. **Listening and Grammar.** Tag questions (such as "You like this, *don't you?*") are used only in spoken conversations. Listen to an interview on the radio or watch a conversation scene from a video. Can you hear any tag questions? What are the most common tag questions that you hear?

4. **Speaking and Grammar.** Make a list of 5 things you think you know about a classmate, a friend, or your teacher. Don't choose things that everyone already knows (for example, physical appearance, nationality) and don't choose things the person has told you. Instead, make some guesses about the person. Try to make some verbs positive and some negative. Use tags with all your questions.

5. **Project.** Shakespeare is a writer who has had a major influence on Western culture, and many students today study Shakespeare. Research a writer who has influenced your native country and culture. Give a short presentation to your class. Give examples of how this writer has influenced you and your culture.

Grammar Explanations

This section contains the same grammar explanations that are found on the CD-ROM. They are included here for your quick reference. To view the animated presentation, go to the Grammar section of Unit A.4 in the CD-ROM course.

Grammar 1: Tag Questions

1. We use **tag questions** to check information.
   Nick: I know you, **don't I?**
   Talia: Yes. I'm Talia Santos.

   In this example, Nick thinks he knows Talia. He uses a tag question to see if he is right. *I know you, don't I?* means *I know you, right?*

2. We can also use tag questions to make a comment. We don't expect an answer. We usually think the person is going to agree with us.
   Talia: I told you the truth, **didn't I?** I'll be fair.
   Really. You can trust me.

   In this example, Talia expects Nick to agree with her. She is not really asking Nick a question.

3. A tag question is made of a statement and a tag.
   Nick: **I know you, don't I?**

   I know you is the statement. And *don't I?* is the tag.

   Notice that the subject of the tag is the same as the subject of the statement.
   Nick: **You** were in my class, weren't **you?**

   We use pronouns only in the tag.
   Amy: Nick was in your class, wasn't **he?**

   We do **NOT** say: ~~Nick was in your class, wasn't Nick?~~

Statement	Tag
I know you,	don't I?

4. When the statement is **affirmative**, the tag is **negative**.
   You **were** in my class, **weren't** you?

   You were in my class is affirmative. The tag, *weren't you?*, is negative.

   Notice that the tag for *I am* is *aren't I?*
   I'm right, **aren't I?**

5. When the statement is **negative**, the tag is **affirmative**.
   You **weren't** in my class, **were** you?

   You weren't in my class is negative. The tag, *were you?*, is affirmative.

Tag Questions

Statement	Tag
affirmative	negative
negative	affirmative
noun or pronoun subject	subject always a pronoun
a form of *be*	a form of *be*
don't or *doesn't*	*do* or *does*
a verb without auxiliary	a form of *do*
same tense as in tag	same tense as in statement

6. The tag always has a form of the verb *be* or an auxiliary verb. Auxiliary verbs are sometimes called *helping* verbs. They are the verbs *do, be,* and *have,* and modals like *can, could, should,* and *will.* If the statement has the verb *be* or an auxiliary verb, we use the same verb in the tag.

   Notice that the tense is the same for the verb in both the statement and the verb in the tag.
   You**'re** a big soccer fan, **aren't** you?
   You **don't** trust me, **do** you?
   We **can** meet again, **can't** we?

   If the statement does not have either a form of *be* or an auxiliary verb, we must use a form of *do* in the tag. Remember, the tense is the same for both the verb in the statement and the verb in the tag.
   I **know** you, **don't** I?
   We **studied** together for the final, **didn't** we?

Grammar 2: Adjectives and Adverbs

1. We use adjectives to describe a person or a thing.
   Nick: Dr. Custer was a **tough** teacher.
   Her class was **difficult,** but it was **good.**

2. Adjectives can go before the noun.
   She was a **tough teacher.**

   Adjectives can also go after the verb *be* or after non-action verbs such as *look* or *seem.*
   Talia: The charges **are serious.**
   It doesn't **look good.**

3. We use adverbs to describe an action. **Adverbs of manner** describe *how* something is done.
   Nick: I speak **fluently.**
   Talia: Don't judge me so **quickly.**

4. Adverbs of manner usually go after the verb. But they never go between a verb and its object.

> Nick plays soccer.
> Nick **plays** soccer **well**.
>
> We do **NOT** say: ~~Nick plays well soccer.~~

5. Most adverbs of manner end in *-ly*.

> He decided **quickly**.

But some adverbs of manner do not end in *-ly*.

> He did **well**.

And some adverbs of manner have the same form as adjectives.

> He was a **hard** worker.
> He worked **hard**.

Remember, *hardly* is a word, but it is not the adverb form of *hard*. We say, *I work hard. Hardly* means *almost not at all*. It goes before the verb: *I hardly work*.

Lately is also a word, but it is not the adverb form of *late*. We say *I got there late. Lately* has a similar meaning to *recently*, and we use it with the present perfect.

Adjective	Adverb
fluent	fluently
quick	quickly
fair	fairly
different	differently

Adjective	Adverb
good	well
hard	hard
early	early
late	late
wrong	wrong
right	right

Grammar 3: Articles

1. We use the articles *a* or *an* when we talk about singular indefinite nouns. This means that you are not talking about one specific person, place, or thing.

> **Nick:** We were in a class together.

In this example, Nick has not identified which specific class. It's just one of many classes.

We cannot use *a* before a plural noun.

Remember, we use *a* before **consonant sounds**.

> a class
> a university class

We use *an* before **vowel sounds**.

> an English class
> an honest man

2. We use the article *the* when we talk about singular or plural definite nouns. This means that we are talking about a specific person, place, or thing.

> **Talia:** That's right, **the Shakespeare class**.

In this example, Talia is talking about a **specific** class— the Shakespeare class.

> **Talia:** Nick, **the charges** are serious.

In this example, Talia talking about the specific charges against Nick.

3. Very often, we use *a* or *an* the **first time** we mention something. We use *the* the **next time** we mention it.

> **Nick:** We were in **an English literature class** together, weren't we?
> **Talia:** That's right, **the Shakespeare class**.

4. We use *the* when a person, place, or thing is **unique**. This means there is **only one**.

> **Amy:** Is Nick **the captain** of his team?

Amy says *the captain* because there is **only one** captain on a team.

> **Talia:** I want **the true story**.

Talia says *the true story* because there can be many stories, but **only one** true story.

B.1 | Nick's Explanation

🎧 **A. Listen to Track 13.** *Talia is talking to Nick about the scandal. Two words in each line are in the wrong order. Underline the words.*

1. **Talia:** You're one of the <u>best country's</u> soccer players . . .

2. **Nick:** Of course, some people think that's not a such great achievement.

3. **Nick:** I hardly could walk; I certainly couldn't play.

4. **Nick:** I sat out the first-round qualifying match because I had a ankle sprained.

5. **Nick:** How anybody can believe such a ridiculous thing?

6. **Talia:** Then you can explain the tape?

🎧 **B. Listen to Track 14.** *Nick is talking with Talia, Coach Haskins, and Dean Bishop. Complete the sentences from the dialog.*

1. **Nick:** Why _____would I do_____ something so stupid?

2. **Nick:** Some TV station _____ that I deliberately sat out a game.

3. **Nick:** This is an old friend of mine from college, Talia Santos. She _____ *Newsline.*

4. **Coach:** Look, I don't think it's _____ idea to talk to the media right now.

5. **Nick:** Why would anybody _____ to me?

6. **Coach:** They _____ the game next week.

🎧 **C. Listen to Track 15.** *You will hear advice for dealing with a sprained ankle. Match the beginnings and endings of the sentences.*

_d_ 1. First, carefully remove

____ 2. Next, compress the ankle by wrapping

____ 3. Then apply

____ 4. After that, elevate

____ 5. If you are in a lot of pain, take

____ 6. After 30 minutes, try to stand, but don't put

____ 7. Continue to apply

a. too much weight on the ankle.

b. an ice bag.

c. an over-the-counter pain medication.

d. your shoe and sock.

e. the ankle so that it is higher than your heart.

f. an ice bag on the ankle for 20 minutes, every 2 hours throughout the next day.

g. an elastic bandage 2 times around the sprained ankle.

Vocabulary

See Appendix 2 to review the vocabulary terms.

Nick's teammates are talking about the rumor involving Nick and what might happen to their team. Complete the sentences with the correct expression with get. *Be sure to use the appropriate tense.*

get along	get it	get real	get over	get through
get out of	get going	get ahead	get it together	get carried away

1. **Steve:** What's going on? I just don't _____ get it _____ ! If Nick didn't take a bribe, then who is trying to make it look like he did? And why?!

2. **Dean:** Do you think one of the players on another team could have done this to Nick?

   Allan: I don't know. Nick usually _____ with all the players in the league.

3. **Brian:** _____, Allan! Anyone could be doing this to Nick, even one of his friends!

4. **Colin:** Nick shouldn't be talking to reporters about this rumor.

   Hyung: It's too late—he can't _____ it now. He's already talked to some *Newsline* reporter.

5. **Ray:** Nick's such an important part of our team. We'll lose without him!

   Carlos: Now, don't _____, Ray! We don't know for sure that Nick won't be able to play!

6. **Dan:** I agree with Carlos. Nick can _____ this. He's a tough guy and he can handle these reporters.

7. **Christian:** If Nick really is guilty, will the fans ever _____ it? Will they be angry at the whole team?!

8. **Johnny:** Nick wouldn't hurt his career! He knows no athlete has ever _____ in the sports world by taking a bribe.

9. **Roshwan:** Well, we can't live in the past. We've got to _____. We may have to unite and win without Nick.

10. **Joe:** Rosh is right! We'd better _____. Come on, let's go! Let's start practice right now.

Non-Action Verbs

Complete the selections from Talia's personal journal. Fill in the missing verbs. Use a simple tense (for non-action verbs) or a continuous tense.

| Monday | Tony finally **(understand)** _understands_ how much I **(want)** _____ to be a reporter. He told me I could have the Crawford story if I found something big. The question is: **(he/really/mean)** _____ it?

| Tuesday | I **(no/have)** _____ time to write today! Too busy!

| Wednesday | Well, I talked to Nick. At first, he didn't trust me. I **(no/think)** _____ he has something to hide; I **(think)** _____ famous athletes often **(no/trust)** _____ reporters. Maybe he **(think)** _____ I was trying to use our friendship to get ahead in my career?? I **(like)** _____ Nick and I **(no/want)** _____ to see him get hurt. But I need a good story! ☺ Anyway, he finally agreed to tell me his side of the story.

| Thursday | Nick introduced me to his coach. Coach Haskins **(look)** _____ like a really nice guy. It seems like Nick **(have)** _____ really cool teammates, too! I still **(feel)** _____ strange about the tape, though. I **(need)** _____ to find out the truth!

| Friday | Tonight I went out to a new restaurant with Amy. Pizzaro's Pizzeria is such a great restaurant! The pasta dishes **(taste)** _____ superb! The waiter **(put)** _____ some of my spaghetti in a "doggie bag" for me to take home. In fact, I **(have)** _____ some more of it right now!

Modals of Request

A. Complete the conversations. Circle the appropriate phrase.

1. **Jenny: Would you mind to lend me / Would you please lending me /** (**Would you mind lending me**) your notes for last Tuesday's journalism class?

2. **Phil from the audio department: Would you mind / Can you mind / Could you please** bringing me another copy of the Crawford tape?

3. **Talia: Can I to ask you / Can I ask you / Can I asking you** a few more questions? I need to know more about this injury.

4. **Viet:** Since you're going to the audio department, would you **return / returned / returns** this tape player to them?

5. **Phil MacGregor, audio expert: Would / Will / Could** you mind telling me where you got this tape?

6. **Coach Haskins:** Hey, Dean! **Will you get me / Would you get please me / Would you mind to get me** a cup of coffee from the vending machine?

B. Now match each request in Exercise A with the best response.

  _6_ **Dean:** Sure. No problem, Coach.

  _____ **Talia:** Sure. I'll leave my notebook in your mailbox.

  _____ **Talia:** I'm afraid I can't tell you that. I'm not allowed to reveal my source.

  _____ **Clara:** Sorry, I can't. I'm not actually going to the audio department.

  _____ **Amy:** Not at all. I'll be down in a few minutes.

  _____ **Nick:** Sure, but can you wait a few minutes? Practice will be over soon.

BONUS
Think of 2 requests you would like to make. Write the person and the request below. Use different forms of request.

  EXAMPLE: person: _____My teacher_____ request: _____Can I give you my homework tomorrow?_____

1. person: _____ request: _____

2. person: _____ request: _____

Grammar 3

So and *Such*

A. *A reporter from* Newsline *is doing a background story about Nick. She's talking to people who knew Nick in the past. Make sentences using* such *and* so *and the given words. Put the verb in the past tense and add an article* (a or an) *where necessary.*

Nick's college English literature professor

1. Nick / be / bright and serious student

   Nick was such a bright and serious student.

2. Nick and his friends / study / hard

   Nick and his friends studied so hard.

Nick's neighbor from his childhood home

3. Harold and Mary Crawford / be / good influences on Nick

   _____

4. That's why / Nick / be / honest child.

   _____

Nick's first girlfriend

5. Nick / be / sweet / on our first date.

   _____

6. He / bring me / beautiful flowers.

   _____

Philip, Nick's best friend when he was a child

7. Nick / wanted / be on the national team / much

   _____

8. Sometimes I / get / mad at him / for being / competitive player

   _____

   (*Hint:* There are two places to use *such* or *so*.)

9. Nick / get / busy / when he / become a professional

   _____

B. *What do you think people from your past might say about you? Make sentences using* so *or* such.

EXAMPLE: Naomi was such a quiet girl. (My high school teacher)

1. _____

2. _____

Language Functions

See Appendix 3 to review the language function charts.

A. *Tony is giving some orders and making some requests. Complete the conversations by writing each order or request in a different way. Fill in each blank with 1 word.*

1. Tony: **Finish this story by tonight.**

I _____ you to finish this story by tonight.

Andrea: Sure, Tony. No problem.

2. Tony: **Can you ask Amy to come and see me?**

When you have a _____, could you ask Amy to come and see me?

Alex: Well, actually, I don't know where she is.

3. Tony: **I need you to get a copy of Nick's bank statement.**

Get a copy of Nick's bank statement for me, _____.

Amy: OK, no problem. I'm on it, Tony.

4. Tony: **Can you give this to John Connelly?**

Would you _____ giving this to John Connelly?

Ms. Boyd: I'd be glad to.

B. *Complete the conversations with orders or requests and responses. There is more than 1 possible answer.*

1. Coach Haskins: (give / Nick's medical report) Would you mind giving me Nick's medical report?

Team doctor (*agreeing*): _____

2. Tony: (find out / does Talia know Nick well) _____

Amy (*refusing*): _____

3. Talia: (tell / the truth) _____

Nick (*agreeing*): _____

4. Tony: (find out / the report is ready) _____

Amy (*delaying*): _____

Application Activities

Study Tip
Listen in class. Write down other students' questions and the teacher's responses. After class, review your notes.

1. **Grammar.** Review the different ways you know to make requests. Write as many ways as you can to say: *Lend me your book.* Which are formal? Which are informal?

2. **Vocabulary.** In the story, Talia gets a chance to talk to a famous athlete (Nick Crawford). If you could interview a famous person, who would it be? What questions would you ask? What do you think the person might say? Try to use "get" expressions, if you can.

3. **Writing.** Have you ever been part of a "team," such as a sports team, a band or orchestra, a drama club, or a sales team? Write a paragraph about your experience.

4. **Speaking.** Ask 2 or 3 people what kinds of injuries they have had from sports, from other activities, or from accidents. What did they do about them? Were the treatments effective for them?

5. **Project.** Go to a health website. Find out the best way to treat a minor physical problem, such as a common cold, a burn, or an insect bite. Do people in your country have different methods of treating the problem? Report to the class what you found out.

Grammar Explanations

This section contains the same grammar explanations that are found on the CD-ROM. They are included here for your quick reference. To view the animated presentation, go to the Grammar section of Unit B.1 in the CD-ROM course.

Grammar 1: Non-Action Verbs

1. Some verbs express **actions**. We can use them in the simple form or in the continuous form (verb + -*ing*).
    Talia **works** for *Newsline*.
    At the moment, she**'s working** on the Nick Crawford story.

2. Some verbs do not express actions. These verbs are called **non-action** (or stative) verbs. We usually do not use them in the continuous form, even when we are talking about something that is happening right now.
    Talia **wants** an explanation **right now**.
    We do **NOT** say: ~~Talia is wanting an explanation right now.~~

3. **Non-action verbs** can express many things:
    They can express **feelings**. Some examples are *feel, like, love,* and *hate.*
    Nick **loves** soccer.
    They can express **thoughts**. Some examples are *think, understand, mean, know, believe,* and *remember.*
    Coach: I **know** all about it.
    Nick: What **do** you **mean**?
    Non-action verbs can also express **needs** and **preferences**. Some examples are *need, prefer,* and *want.*
    Coach: I **don't want** to worry you.
    We can also use **non-action verbs** to talk about **possessions**. Some examples are *have* and *own.*
    Talia **has** a good job.
    We also use **non-action verbs** to talk about the 5 **senses** (sight, sound, smell, touch, and taste). Some examples of these are *see, look, hear, sound, smell, feel,* and *taste.*
    Talia: It **sounds** like you.
    Nick **looks** worried.

4. The verb *be* is usually a non-action verb. It describes how someone or something always is.
    Nick: This **is** an old friend of mine from college.

5. Some verbs can have **both an action and a non-action** meaning.
    Talia **is having** breakfast.
    In this sentence *have* means *eat,* and it is an action verb.
    Talia **has** a microwave oven.
    In this sentence *have* means *own,* and it is a non-action verb.

Other verbs that can be action or non-action	
Action Amy **is smelling** the flowers.	**Non-action** They **smell** great.
Action The coach **is thinking** about Nick.	**Non-action** He **doesn't think** they can win without him.

Grammar 2: Modals of Request

1. We can make a **request** with *will, can, would,* or *could* plus a subject and the base form of the verb.
    Will you **come** here for a minute?
    Can you **come** here for a minute?
    Would you **come** here for a minute?
    Could you **come** here for a minute?

2. *Will* and *can* are **informal**.
    For example, Nick and the coach know each other very well. They have a relaxed, friendly relationship. Nick makes a request with *can.*
    Nick: Coach! **Can** you come here for a minute?
    Could and *would* are more **polite**.
    For example, the coach is speaking to Dean, Nick, and Talia. He doesn't know Talia. The coach makes a request with *would.*
    Coach: **Would** you excuse us, please?

3. We can also make requests more **polite** by using *please.*
    Please can go before the base form of the verb.
    Would you **please call** me tonight?
    Please can also go at the end of the request.
    Coach: Would you excuse us, **please**?

4. Another way to make a **polite** request is to start the sentence with *Would you mind* plus the gerund. Remember, the gerund is formed with the verb + -*ing*.
    Would you mind coming here for a minute?
    We do not usually use *please* with *Would you mind . . . ?*

5. We usually **agree** to a request with words like *yes, sure, certainly,* and *of course.*
    Nick: Can you come here for a minute?
    Coach: Sure.
    We agree to a *Would you mind . . . ?* request with *Not at all.*
    Coach: Would you mind excusing us for a minute?
    Talia: Not at all.

Not at all means *It's OK. I'll do it.*

A *yes* answer to a request with *Would you mind* means *It's not OK. I won't do it.*

When we say *no* to a request, we usually **apologize and give a reason**.

Talia: Amy, can you come here for a minute?
Amy: **Sorry, I'm on the phone.**

We never use *could* and *would* in short answers to requests.

Amy: Could you help me carry this?
Talia: **Sure.**

We do **NOT** say: ~~Yes, I could.~~

Grammar 3: *So* and *Such*

1. We use ***so*** and ***such*** to make a statement ***stronger***. For example, we can say:
   Talia works hard.

But we can also make a stronger statement and say:
   Talia works **so** hard.
This means that Talia works very hard.

Here's another example. We can say:
   Talia is a hard worker.

But we can make a stronger statement and say:
   Talia is **such** a hard worker.
This means that Talia is a very hard worker.

2. We use ***so*** before an adjective or an adverb.
   Nick: Why would I do something **so stupid**?
   Talia works **so hard**.

3. We use ***such*** before an adjective plus a noun. The noun can be singular or plural.
   Nick: How can anyone believe **such a ridiculous thing**?

You need an indefinite article (*a* or *an*) before the adjective if the noun is singular.

B.2 | Bad News

🎧 **A. Listen to Track 16.** *Tony is talking with Talia and Amy at the* Newsline *office. Complete this part of the conversation.*

Talia: But except for that tape, we have no

(1)_____ . . .

Tony: We (2)_____ no proof. We

(3)_____ it now. Amy, tell her.

Amy: I'm sorry, Talia. The audit of Nick's bank account

(4)_____ in. He

(5)_____ $50,000 in his bank account

a (6)_____ the qualifying match.

Talia: Oh, my gosh. What? Let me see that . . . I'm not going to (7)_____.

There might be a good (8)_____ for this.

🎧 **B. Listen to Track 17.** *Tony is still talking with Talia about the story. Check (✓) the phrases you hear.*

1. ✓ You can keep investigating. ____ You ought to keep investigating.

2. ____ We're going with this story tonight. ____ We might go with this story tonight.

3. ____ I keep telling myself we're missing something. ____ I keep telling you we're missing something.

4. ____ You just may be too trusting to be a reporter. ____ You are just too trusting to be a reporter.

5. ____ Are you sure you're all right working on this by yourself? ____ Are you sure you're all right working on this without any help?

6. ____ I promised myself I'd do a good job. ____ I promised you I'd do a good job.

🎧 **C. Listen to Track 18.** *You will hear part of a radio talk show about the private lives of entertainers. Complete the script. Circle the correct words or phrases.*

Caller: Hello. I'm a big movie **fan /(buff)**, and I read all the **entertainment / gossip** magazines. I love reading about movie stars and their private lives. Ordinary people want to know **what the stars are doing / what the stars are up to**—that's only **natural / normal**! But on the other hand, I can understand why some stars get angry when reporters and photographers **reveal / tell** all their embarrassing secrets. **Anyone / Everyone** needs a little privacy . . . even movie stars!

Vocabulary

See Appendix 2 to review the vocabulary terms.

Complete the conversation with the correct expression with feel. *Be careful: Sometimes you have to change the verb form of* feel *or make a question.*

feel for (someone)	feel free	feel funny
feel like (doing something)	feel like (something)	feel (somebody) out
feel up to (something)	feel (your)self	

James: Let's get a group together and go dancing tonight. Hand me your cell phone; I'm going to call Nick.

Aidan: I don't know if he'll (1)_____*feel up to*_____ going out. He's having a really hard time these days, with the rumor going around and everything.

James: I know. I really (2)_____ him. I wouldn't want to go through what he's going through. But let's ask him anyway. It just might make him feel better.

Aidan: Hey, Nick! Do you (3)_____ going dancing tonight?

Nick: That sounds great. I haven't been (4)_____ these days. Maybe this will get the "old Nick" back. Maybe I'll even meet someone.

James: I don't think you should talk to that reporter. She may be a spy!

Nick: I'm a good judge of character. And I think I've gotten pretty good at (5)_____ people _____. Talia just seems like someone I can trust.

Aidan: Are you going to speak with her again?

Nick: Yes, of course. I told her to (6)_____ to call me if she has any more questions.

James: I don't know. I (7)_____ about the whole thing. Just be careful, Nick.

Grammar 1

Gerunds as Subjects and Objects

A. Complete the entries from Talia's personal journal. Fill in the blanks with the correct form of the verbs or nouns in parentheses. Add prepositions where necessary.

1. I (**enjoy / work**) ____enjoy working____ on the Crawford story.
2. It's not easy though. I (**not recall / feel**) _____ this emotional on a story before.
3. I'm (**look forward / go**) _____ on a vacation after this story is finally over!
4. Why would Nick do it? (**take / bribe**) _____ doesn't make sense.
5. Why would Nick (**risk / get caught**) _____?
6. If there is real proof, I'll have to believe it. I'll have to (**start / admit**) _____ that Nick is a different person.

B. Now write sentences about yourself. Use a gerund with each verb.

1. (**enjoy**) _____
2. (**miss**) _____
3. (**keep**) _____

Grammar 2

Modals of Possibility

A. Complete the conversations. Use may, might, *or* could *and the words in parentheses. Use each modal at least once.*

1. **Dean:** Coach Haskins isn't in his office. Where is he?

   Nick: I don't know. He (**be in the exercise room**) _____might be in the exercise room._____.

2. **Tony:** Amy doesn't look too good today. What's wrong?

   Talia: I'm not really sure. She (**have a cold**) _____.

3. **Talia:** Can you and John meet us in the conference room at 3:00?

   Andy: I don't know yet. We (**have another appointment**) _____ at 3:00.

4. **Jorge:** There's a cell phone on my desk. Whose is it?

   Ryan: Hmm. I don't know. It (**belong to Talia**) _____.

B. *Give short answers to the following questions. Use* may, might, *or* could *and a verb if necessary.*

1. **Talia:** Do you think Carla will get a promotion?

   Amy: I can't say. She _____.

2. **Ryan:** Do you think Talia likes John?

   Jorge: I don't think so, but she _____.

3. **Celia:** Is it too late to call Amy?

   Talia: Gee, it's 10 o'clock. _____.

Grammar 3

Reflexive Pronouns

A. Friends and co-workers of people at Newsline *reveal surprising gossip about each other (and themselves). Fill in the correct reflexive pronoun.*

myself	yourself	yourselves	itself
herself	themselves	ourselves	himself

1. **Talia:** You know what? Amy mumbles to _____herself_____ when she's writing essays for her journalism class.

2. **Tony's wife:** You may not know this about Tony—Tony sings to _____ when he's in the shower.

3. **Dean:** Did you hear? After Nick left practice, Coach Haskins told everyone on the team, "Prepare _____ to play without Nick. I think that the Soccer Federation is not going to let him play in the qualifying match."

4. **Talia:** I hate to say this, but I'm not 100% sure I can handle the Crawford investigation by _____.

5. **Carlos:** Tony called John into his office and told him, "If Talia can't accept the truth about Nick Crawford *by next week*, you'll have to do the story _____."

6. **Nick:** Dean spends too much time with his dog. When Dean leaves the room even for 1 minute, his dog cries to _____. Poor thing!

B. Which one of these things do you do? Write a sentence for each one you do.

1. Talk or whisper to yourself

2. Sing, whistle, or hum to yourself

3. Buy yourself something nice when you've had a hard week

EXAMPLE: I sing to myself when I'm driving my car.

1. _____

2. _____

3. _____

Language Functions

See Appendix 3 to review the language function charts.

A. Read each sentence. Then write a sentence with a similar meaning, using the word in parentheses. Be sure the use the appropriate tense.

1. It's possible that we'll go to Rocco's Pizzeria later. **(may)**

    We may go to Rocco's Pizzeria later.

2. I might have to work late tonight. **(possible)**

    _____

3. We may go camping this weekend. **(chance)**

    _____

4. There's a chance that my partner and I will live in Europe in the future. **(could)**

    _____

5. I could be an English teacher someday. **(likely)**

    _____

B. Now write some sentences about yourself. Use these expressions: It's possible that . . . / There's a chance that . . . / It's likely that . . .

1. What are you going to do tonight?

_____

2. How about this weekend—what are you going to do?

_____

3. What kind of job will you be doing in 5 years' time?

_____

4. Do you plan to live in another country someday?

_____

Application Activities

Study Tip
Review the Language Functions charts on pages 116–122. Write dialogs with the new phrases. Act them out!

1. **Listening and Grammar.** Listen to today's news on the TV, radio, or Internet. Listen for modals of possibility. Write down at least 5 examples. Try to write down as much of the sentence as you can. If possible, record the program so you can play it back if you miss part of the sentence.

2. **Writing.** In the story, Talia says, "Things aren't always as they seem." Explain the meaning of this expression. Give an example.

3. **Listening and Discussion.** Talk with people about a current TV news story. What is it about? Do you believe what the people in the story say? Would you say you are a *skeptical* person? Why or why not?

4. **Speaking.** Talk with people about their future plans and possibilities. Ask questions like these: *Do you think that . . . ? Is it possible that . . . ? Is there a chance that . . . ?*

5. **Project.** Find a newspaper or online news service from your native country. Choose an article that discusses something you think people who aren't from your country should learn about. Write down the 5 W's for the story and share it with a classmate.

Grammar Explanations

This section contains the same grammar explanations that are found on the CD-ROM. They are included here for your quick reference. To view the animated presentation, go to the Grammar section of Unit B.2 in the CD-ROM course.

Grammar 1: Gerunds as Subjects and Objects

1. A **gerund** is the **base form of the verb + -ing**. Remember, when we add *-ing* to a verb, there are often spelling changes.
   play—play**ing**
   make—mak**ing**
   shop—shopp**ing**

2. A **gerund** acts like a noun and it can be the subject of a sentence.
   Amy: **Gambling** may be a problem for Nick.

   A gerund is always **singular**. It is followed by the third person singular form (*he, she, it*) of the verb.
   Talia: **Making** money **is** not a problem for him.

3. A **gerund** can also be the object of a verb.
   Tony: You can **keep investigating**.

   In the example, *investigating* is the object of the verb *keep*. There are many verbs, like *keep*, that are followed by a gerund.

Some verbs that are followed by a gerund		
avoid	enjoy	finish
keep	practice	prefer
quit	risk	stop

4. A **gerund** can also follow a preposition, a word like *about, after, before, for, of, on, with,* and *without*.
   Tony: **After looking** at this bank statement, we have no choice.

Grammar 2: Modals of Possibility

1. We use words like *may*, *might*, and *could* to talk about possibilities—things we are not 100 percent sure about.
   Amy: Gambling **may** be a problem for him.

   Amy isn't sure that gambling is a problem for Nick, but she thinks it is a possibility.
   Amy: He **might** owe a lot of people money.

   Amy isn't sure that Nick owes a lot of money, but she thinks it is a possibility.
   Talia: This **could** all be a mistake.

   Talia isn't sure that it is all a mistake, but she thinks it is possibly a mistake.

2. We can use *may*, *might*, and *could* to talk about **possibility in the present**.
   Nick **might** be guilty.

We can also use these modals to talk about **possibility in the future**.
   Our competition **may** beat us to the story.

Remember, when we are 100 percent **certain about the future**, we use *be going to* or *will*.
   Talia **is not going to** stop investigating.
   She **won't** quit.

3. Notice that *may*, *might*, and *could* are followed by the base form of the verb.
   Amy: Gambling **may be** a problem for him. He **might owe** a lot of money.
   Talia: This **could be** a mistake.

4. We use only *may not* and *might not* in **negative** statements. We do not use *could not*.
   Tony: It **may not** always make sense.

   We do **NOT** say: ~~It could not always make sense.~~

   We do not use contractions for *may not* and *might not*.

   We do **NOT** say: ~~mayn't~~ or ~~mightn't~~

5. To ask **questions** about present possibility, we usually use *could*, the present, or expressions like *Do you think*. We do not usually use *may* or *might*.
   Amy: **Could** Nick be innocent? **Is** he honest? **Do you think** he's telling the truth?
   Talia: He might be.

   To ask about future possibility, we often use *will* or *be going to*.
   Amy: Talia, **will** you be in the office tomorrow morning?
   Talia: I'm not sure. I might be out.

6. In **short answers** to *yes/no* questions about possibility, we use *may*, *might*, or *could* alone.
   Amy: Do you think Nick owes a lot of money?
   Tony: He **might**.

   When a form of *be* is the main verb in the question, use *be* in the answer.
   Amy: **Is** Nick guilty?
   Tony: He **may be**.

Grammar 3: Reflexive Pronouns

1. We use **reflexive pronouns** when the subject and the object of a sentence refer to **the same person**.
   Talia: **I** promised **myself** I'd do a good job.

   In this sentence the **subject** (*I*) is Talia. The **object** (*myself*) is also Talia. The subject and the object are the same person: Talia. So, Talia promised Talia. In other words, Talia promised herself.
   Talia promised Talia.
   Talia promised **herself**.

2. These are the reflexive pronouns: *myself, yourself, himself, herself, itself, ourselves, yourselves,* and *themselves.*

Notice that *you* has two reflexive pronouns. Use ***yourself*** when you are speaking to 1 person. Use ***yourselves*** when you are speaking to more than 1 person.

Alex: Hey, Talia, do you ever talk to yourself?
Kim: Hey, guys, do you ever talk to yourselves?

Reflexive Pronouns
I looked at **myself** in the mirror.
You looked at **yourself** in the mirror.
He looked at **himself** in the mirror.
She looked at **herself** in the mirror.
It looked at **itself** in the mirror.
We looked at **ourselves** in the mirror.
You looked at **yourselves** in the mirror.
They looked at **themselves** in the mirror.

3. We use ***by* plus a reflexive pronoun** to mean *alone* or *without any help.*

Tony: Are you sure you'll be all right working on this by yourself?

B.3 An Endorsement Deal

Listening

🎧 **A. Listen to Track 19.** *Talia is talking to Nick at the health club. Cross out the extra word in each line from the conversation.*

1. **Talia:** There you are! Nick, ~~when~~ are you going to stop lying to me?

2. **Nick:** Hello, Talia. And how are you? Where would you like to have a seat?

3. **Talia:** No, actually, I would prefer to stand.

4. **Nick:** OK. Whatever. So now what's been going on?

5. **Talia:** This! $50,000 has appeared in your bank account just before the qualifying match. $50,000!

6. **Nick:** So what?

7. **Talia:** So? So that's exactly the amount of money they say you accepted for throwing out that game.

8. **Nick:** It's also the exact amount of money I got for endorsing a great new line of athletic shoes.

🎧 **B. Listen to Track 20.** *Nick is telling Talia what happened when he met Jackie Baker. Complete the conversation between Nick and Jackie.*

Jackie: Excuse me. (1)_____ Nick Crawford?

Nick: Yes, that's right. (2)_____?

Jackie: No. (3)_____, that is. I'm Jackie Baker. I'm the VP of (4)_____ for Kicks Shoes.

Nick: Uh-huh.

Jackie: And I have a very interesting (5)_____ for you.

Nick: Keep going. I'm (6)_____.

Jackie: Why don't we (7)_____ at (8)_____ tomorrow? Let's say, 12:30. We can have lunch nearby, and I'll (9)_____ you all about the (10)_____.

🎧 *C. Listen to Track 21. You will hear some product jingles. Find the words that rhyme (have the same sound).*

Sweet-Aid

pink rhymes with _____drink_____

wow rhymes with _____

Laura's Secret

fine rhymes with _____

compare rhymes with _____

Auntie Nell Donuts

be rhymes with _____

Vocabulary

See Appendix 2 to review the vocabulary terms.

A. Put an N *by the nouns and a* V *by the verbs in the box.*

analyze V	appointment	criticize	combination	announce
develop	pressure	proposal	react	recommend

B. Nick told Talia about his mysterious meeting with Jackie Baker. Later, Talia is imagining what Nick and Jackie might have said. Complete the conversation. Use the words from the box in Exercise A. Change the verbs to the appropriate tenses.

Jackie: Thanks for keeping our (1)____appointment____, Nick. As I told you yesterday, I have a

(2)_____ to present to you. A few days ago, Kicks, the athletic shoe

company, (3)_____ that they're looking for a talented athlete to do a

commercial. I (4)_____ you because you're talented, smart, funny, and

handsome. That (5)_____ of qualities sells products!

Nick: It sounds great, Jackie, but I don't know. Maybe I should run this deal by an agent first.

Jackie: I don't want to put too much (6)_____ on you, but we're considering some

other athletes, too. The company has already (7)_____ the ideas for the

commercial. They want to start filming very soon. You have until 4:00 p.m. to decide.

Nick: 4:00 p.m.?! There's no way I could get an agent to help me before then! I don't know,

Jackie. Working with an agent is important. It's an agent's job to (8)_____

endorsement deals. They make sure the company is being fair.

Jackie: Doesn't $50,000 for a few hours of your time sound fair? I don't mean to

(9)_____ you, Nick, but you're thinking too much about this. You'd be crazy

to miss this opportunity—and you *will* miss it if you wait too long.

Nick: I didn't mean to (10)_____ that way. I guess I'm just naturally skeptical. But

you're right. I don't need an agent to help me make this decision. OK—I'll do it!

Grammar 1

Study Tip
Volunteer! Say 3 things in class every day. Ask questions.

Past Continuous

A. *The employees at* Newsline *decided to play a little trick on Tony.*
(It was April 1—April Fools' Day—a day when people often play tricks on each other). Complete the story. Fill in the blanks with the correct form of the verbs in parentheses. Choose the simple past or the past continuous.

When Tony (1) (**walk**) _____walked_____ into the room, no one

(2) (**work**) _____. Talia (3) (**watch**) _____ a DVD

when Tony (4) (**approach**) _____ her desk. When Tony

(5) (**look**) _____ around the room, Ms. Boyd

(6) (**read**) _____ a romance novel, and Jeremy and Ryan

(7) (**laugh and make**) _____ photocopies of their hands. Jorge

and Amy (8) (**play**) _____ a video game.

Tony (9) (**stop**) _____ and his eyes (10) (**grow**) _____

very large. When Tony (11) (**see**) _____ his staff, he

(12) (**yell**) _____, "What are you doing, people? We've got a 2:00 deadline!"

The *Newsline* employees (13) (**stare**) _____ at him while he

(14) (**yell**) _____. Then everyone (15) (**start**) _____

laughing. And suddenly everyone (16) (**shout**) _____, "April Fool!"

Then they (17) (**go**) _____ back to work.

B. *Write sentences about what you were doing at different times, such as* at 6 o'clock this morning, at 9 o'clock last night, at this time last year, 2 hours ago, 10 minutes ago.

EXAMPLE: __Two hours ago, I was riding on the train._____

1. _____

2. _____

Modals of Preference

Talia, Amy, Josh, and Tom are trying to decide on a good restaurant for dinner tonight. Correct the mistakes in the use of would rather, prefer, *and* would prefer. *Some sentences have no mistakes.*

1. **Tom:** Where should we go for dinner tonight?

   Amy: Hmm. I'd like a nice steak dinner tonight, but I don't have much money.
   What would
   ~~What'd~~ you prefer, Talia?

2. **Talia:** Steak sounds OK. If possible, I wouldn't rather go to a noisy restaurant.

3. **Amy:** Oh, come on, Talia. How about a little excitement tonight? I prefer some entertainment while I eat. I know Tom usually is preferring that, too.

4. **Tom:** Yes, I am prefer that! You know me so well!

5. **Amy:** How about you, Thomas? Do you rather have sports entertainment or music entertainment tonight?

6. **Tom:** Either is all right. What about you, Josh? What you prefer?

7. **Josh:** I don't care about the entertainment. But I'm really not in the mood for a barbecue tonight. I'd prefer some nice seafood, even if it means going to a more expensive restaurant.

8. **Talia:** Seriously, guys. I'd definitely rather having some peace and quiet. No entertainment for me!

9. **Amy:** Maybe we should split up tonight since we prefer different things. Tom and I can go to one place and you two can go to another. Would you preferred that?

10. **Josh:** Yes, I'd, if that's OK with you guys.

Comparative Adjectives

Nick likes to go snowboarding during the off-season. He is shopping for snowboards. Compare the two snowboard models below. Then complete the sentences with the correct comparative form of the adjectives in parentheses.

The Stylin' 4000 ($$$)
Length: 158 cm Width: 24.9 cm

The Big Kahuna ($$$$$)
Length: 168 cm Width: 26.4 cm

- Available in bright colors
- For snowboarders with skill level beginner-intermediate
- Made of a combination of wood and carbon fiber. Weight: 6.5 pounds
- Flexible (board bends easily)
- Control—very good

- Available only in black and white
- For advanced snowboarders
- Made of wood only. Weight: 6 pounds
- Stiff (board does not bend easily)
- Control—difficult; takes an advanced snowboarder

1. **Nick:** Is The Big Kahuna (**cheap**) _____cheaper than_____ The Stylin' 4000?

   Salesperson: No. The Stylin' 4000 is (**expensive**) ___less expensive than___ The Big Kahuna.

2. **Nick:** I don't really like black and white.

   Salesperson: If you'd prefer a (**colorful**) _____more colorful_____ board, The Stylin' 4000 is a better choice.

3. **Nick:** I see that The Stylin' 4000 is (**short**) _____ The Big Kahuna.

   Salesperson: Yes, that's right. It's 10 centimeters shorter.

4. **Nick:** Is The Big Kahuna (**wide**) _____ The Stylin' 4000?

   Salesperson: Yes. Snowboarders who have (**big**) _____ feet prefer The Big Kahuna. The Stylin' 4000 is (**narrow**) _____ than The Kahuna.

5. **Salesperson:** Are you a good snowboarder?

   Nick: I'm pretty good. Why do you ask?

   Salesperson: Snowboarders who use The Big Kahuna are usually (**advanced**) _____ snowboarders who use The Stylin' 4000.

6. **Nick:** Is The Stylin' 4000 (**heavy**) _____ The Big Kahuna?

   Salesperson: Yes, a little. But it is (**stiff**) _____ The Big Kahuna. Because The Stylin' 4000 is (**flexible**) _____, it is also (**easy**) _____ to control.

Language Functions

See Appendix 3 to review the language function charts.

A. *React to each piece of news. Use responses like* Great, How awful, *or* I see *to show your reaction. More than 1 response is possible.*

1. **Your classmate:** There's no English class next week.

   You: _____

2. **Your friend:** Sorry I'm late. The traffic was terrible.

   You: _____

3. **Your roommate:** There was a call for you while you were out.

   You: _____

4. **Your friend:** I was in a little traffic accident last night.

   You: _____

5. **Your colleague at work:** I think I'm going to get a big promotion!

   You: _____

B. *Respond and ask follow-up questions to the pieces of news.*

1. **Your friend:** I went to a movie last night.

   You: _____

2. **Your co-worker:** I went to Max's party last night. It was a terrible party.

   You: _____

3. **Your friend:** I had a job interview this morning.

   You: _____

4. **Your boyfriend/girlfriend:** I don't think we should see each other anymore.

   You: _____

Application Activities

1. **Vocabulary.** One way to increase your vocabulary is to learn verb-noun combinations, such as *combine* (verb) and *combination* (noun). Keep a list of noun-verb combinations. Try to include at least 5 new combinations each week. Write sentences with each pair of words.

2. **Grammar.** Choose 2 similar products (such as electronic items), 2 similar places (such as vacation spots), and 2 similar people (such as popular entertainers). For each pair, write at least 5 sentences to compare them. Use expressions with *-er*, *more*, and *less*.

3. **Writing.** Write about a commercial that you like. Describe it in detail and tell what you like about it. *Or* make up a jingle for a product that you often use (for example, a food item or a cosmetic item) or a place you often visit (for example, a restaurant or amusement park).

4. **Speaking.** Ask someone about recent news in their lives. Suggest different topics if they don't have any news! Possible topics: study, work, family, entertainment, trips, future plans. For each piece of news, try to ask at least 3 follow-up questions.

5. **Project.** Find a newspaper or magazine. Cut out 2 of your favorite ads and bring them to class to share. Present them to your classmates. What are the differences between ads from your country and ads from other countries (like the United States or the United Kingdom)?

Grammar Explanations

This section contains the same grammar explanations that are found on the CD-ROM. They are included here for your quick reference. To view the animated presentation, go to the Grammar section of Unit B.3 in the CD-ROM course.

Grammar 1: Past Continuous

1. We use the **past continuous** to talk about something that was in progress at a specific time in the past. When we use the past continuous, we are not interested in when the activity ended.

    Nick: It was about 10:00. I **was having** something to drink at my health club.

    In the example, Nick started having something to drink before 10:00. We do not know what time he stopped drinking.

The Past Continuous

I **was working**.

You **were working**.

He/She/It **was working**.

We **were working**.

They **were working**.

2. We form the past continuous with **was** or **were** + the base form of the verb + **-ing**.

    I **was working**.
    They **were working**.

    Just as we usually do not use non-action verbs in the present continuous, we do not use non-action verbs in the past continuous.

    We do **NOT** say: ~~Nick was having a headache.~~

3. We can use the **past continuous** with **while** to talk about 2 activities in progress at the same time in the past.

    Nick was playing with the ball. He was talking to Talia.
    Nick **was playing** with the ball **while** he **was talking** to Talia.

    You can also begin the sentence with **while**.
    While Nick **was playing** with the ball, he **was talking** to Talia.

4. Remember, we use the **past continuous** to focus on the activity, not the end of the activity. Often the activity is not finished.

    Talia: What **was** I **saying**?

    In this example, Talia was interrupted by Nick's commercial before she finished talking about the investigation.

We use the **simple past** to focus on the completion of the activity.

What **did** Talia **say**?

In this example, Talia finished talking.

Grammar 2: Modals of Preference

1. We use **prefer** and **would prefer** to talk about preferences—things we like better than other things.
    Nick: Would you like to have a seat?
    Talia: No, I **prefer** to stand.

    Prefer and *would prefer* can be followed by a noun.
    Amy: Would you like a cup of tea?
    Talia: Thanks, but I**'d prefer coffee**.

    Prefer and *would prefer* can also be followed by the gerund. Remember, the gerund is formed with the verb + *-ing*.
    Talia doesn't have time to shop at stores. She **prefers shopping** online.

    Prefer and *would prefer* can also be followed by the infinitive (*to* + the base form of the verb).
    She **prefers to shop** online.

2. We can also make suggestions with *would rather* plus the base form of the verb.
    Talia: I**'d rather pay** her a visit.

    The **negative form** for *would rather* is *would rather not*.
    Talia: I**'d rather not** sit down.

    We do **NOT** say: ~~I wouldn't rather sit down.~~

    We often use **I'd rather not** as a short answer.
    Amy: Maybe you should ask John for help with this story.
    Talia: I**'d rather not**. I want to cover this story by myself.

3. We use *would* to form **questions** with *prefer* and *rather*.
    Nick: Would you **prefer** to sit down?
    Nick: Would you **rather** sit down?

    But we can also use a form of *do* to form **questions** with *prefer*.
    Nick: Do you **prefer** to stand?

Grammar 3: Comparative Adjectives

1. We use **comparative adjectives** to talk about the **differences** between people, places, or things.
    Kicks are **cooler than** your old shoes.
    They're **more comfortable**, too.
    They're **better than** other shoes.

2. There are several ways to **form the comparative**. For **short adjectives**, we usually add *-er*.

    cool—cooler
    short—shorter
    tall—taller

Sometimes, when we add *-er*, there are **spelling changes**.

    nice—nicer
    hot—hotter
    happy—happier

3. A few adjectives have **irregular comparative** forms.

    good—better
    bad—worse

4. For **long adjectives**, we usually form the comparative with *more*.

    Nick: Kicks are more comfortable, too.

We can also make a comparison with *less* (the opposite of *more*) and long adjectives.

    Nick: They're less expensive than they look.

5. Some adjectives have 2 possible comparative forms.

    quiet—quieter OR more quiet

6. We use *than* when we mention the things we are comparing.

    Nick: These shoes are more comfortable than my old shoes.

Notice that we don't always need to use the comparative with *than*. Sometimes it is clear what we are comparing.

    Nick: They're more comfortable, too.

In the example, it is clear that Nick is talking about 2 pairs of shoes. Because Nick doesn't mention the second pair of shoes, he does not use *than*.

B.4 No One by That Name

🎧 **A. Listen to Track 22.** *Talia is talking to the receptionist at the Gower Building. Correct the mistakes in the sentences from the conversation.*

1. I'm here to see ~~Jacqueline~~ ^{Jackie} Baker.

2. I know who you want. Jack Baxter. He's on the third floor, 341.

3. No, I'm here to see Jackie Baker, Mrs. Jackie Baker.

4. There's someone here by that name.

5. This is the Gower Building? 190 Gower Street?

6. Maybe she's still here. Maybe she used to work here.

7. She's a vice president at Kicks Shoes.

8. Now I really don't know who you're talking about.

9. Are you sure you're in the right building?

10. I'm not sure who I am.

11. In fact, I'm not sure about anyone anymore.

🎧 **B. Track 23.** *Talia is calling Nick while the receptionist listens. Complete the phrases with words from the box. You will not use all the words. Then listen to Track 23 and check your answers.*

truth	lunch	card	guest	names
angry	dead	moment	worse	lying
available	voicemail	trouble	memory	

1. My cell phone is _____dead_____.

2. Can I use your phone for a _____?

3. You seem really _____.

4. Someone's in big _____.

5. You seem to have trouble with _____.

6. I used to have a good _____.

7. You've got her business _____.

8. She took me to _____.

9. I'm telling the _____.

10. Well, someone is _____.

🎧 **C. Listen to Track 24.** *You will hear some people asking for directions in an office building. Check (✓) the phrases that you hear.*

Visitor 1

1. ✓ Hello, can I help you?   ____ Hello, how can I help you?

2. ____ I'm looking for the office of William Meyer.   ____ I'm trying to find the office of William Meyer.

3. ____ You'll find MDG Records on the fifth floor.   ____ MDG Records is on the fifth floor.

4. ____ First, could you sign in, please?   ____ First, I need you to sign in, please.

Visitor 2

5. ____ Can I help you find someone's office?   ____ Can I help you find someone?

6. ____ And who is she with?   ____ And she would be with . . . ?

7. ____ Take the C bank of elevators to the twelfth floor.   ____ You'll need to take the C bank of elevators to the twelfth floor.

8. ____ Just a moment. They request that I call up first.   ____ Just a moment. They like me to call up first.

Vocabulary

See Appendix 2 to review the vocabulary terms.

Imagine it is 7 years ago. Talia and Nick are in the university library studying for their English literature course. Complete the conversation with the correct word. Be sure to use the correct tense and form of the verb.

1. **yell, whisper, mutter**

   Nick: Can I borrow your notes?

   Talia: Stop _____yelling_____! I can hear you just fine!

2. **mumble, holler, whisper**

   Nick: Oops, sorry. I always forget to _____

   when I'm in a library.

3. **murmur, mutter, shout**

   Librarian: Excuse me, sir, if you keep _____

   like that, I'm going to have to ask you to leave.

   Talia: I told you!

4. **holler, whisper, mutter**

   Nick: I don't know why the librarian _____ at me.

   I'm not the only one who was making noise.

5. scream, mutter, mumble

Nick: There were some noisy students right outside this window. One of them

_____ something while the librarian was talking to us. I think they were

arguing or something.

6. murmur, shout, mutter

Talia: What _____ you _____ about, Nick? It sounded like you were

complaining about something.

Nick: Oh, I was just complaining about the people outside. Never mind.

7. whisper, yell, mumble

Talia: Why do you want to borrow my notes, anyway? You're the one doing so well in the class!

Nick: I have a hard time understanding our professor. She _____ all the time.

I really can't follow what she's saying most of the time.

8. murmur, shout, scream, whisper

Talia: Well, here are my notes. If you want to borrow anything else, just holler!

Nick: Thanks, but I think I'd better _____!

Grammar 1

Used to

A. *Unscramble the words and phrases to make sentences*
with **used to.** *There are 2 extra words or phrases*
in each group.

1. **Claire: (you / video games / play / using / did /**
   use to / used to) when you were younger?

   Did you use to play video games when you were younger?

   Andy: Did I use to? I still do!

2. **Ms. Boyd:** Tony, when you were younger, did you wear your hair differently?

   Tony: Oh, sure. When I was in college, (**used / I / to / have / long / was / very / did / hair**).

   _____

3. **Josh:** What kind of music did you listen to in high school?

   Talia: When I was in high school, (**used / I / listen / did / to / listening**) to rock music.

   _____

4. **Talia:** When you were a teenager, what did and your friends usually do after school?

   Nick: After school? What do you think? (**played / used to / play / we / did**) soccer for 3 or
   4 hours a day.

   _____

B. *What did you use to do when you were younger? Write 3 sentences.*

EXAMPLE: _I used to play the piano when I was in high school._

1. _____

2. _____

3. _____

Grammar 2

Embedded *Wh-* Questions

A. *Make embedded* wh- *questions using the phrases in the box. Pay attention to word order and add a question mark (?) when necessary. More than one answer may be correct.*

Do you remember . . .	Do you know . . .	Why don't you ask . . .	I wonder . . .
Do you have any idea . . .	I want to know . . .	I don't understand . . .	

1. ***How do you know Nick is innocent?***

    Tony: _I don't understand how you know Nick is innocent._

    Talia: I'm beginning to wonder myself.

2. ***Who is Jackie Baker?***

    Amy: _____

    Talia: No. I'm so confused.

3. ***What did Jackie look like?***

    Talia: _____

    Nick: Not really. I remember she had dark hair but I couldn't tell you much more than that.

4. ***What is the truth?***

    Talia: _____

    Amy: Me, too, Talia. Keep working on it.

5. **Ms. Boyd:** You said Jackie took Nick out to lunch the day of the endorsement deal.

    Talia: Yes. That's what Nick told me.

    Which restaurant did they go to?

    Ms. Boyd: _____

    Talia: Hmmm. That's a good idea. If I know the name of the restaurant, I can check if there are any witnesses who saw them there that day.

B. *Respond to the questions. Use a phrase from the box and the information from each question. Be sure to change the pronouns when necessary. More than 1 answer may be correct.*

I'm not sure	I don't know	I have no idea	I didn't realize
I'm going to find out	I didn't notice	I have trouble believing	

1. **Talia:** When will you know if the tape is fake or real?

   Phil: ___I'm not sure when I'll know if it's fake or real_____. I hope by Friday.

2. **Amy:** How did Nick get injured?

   Talia: I don't know, but _____.

3. **Tony:** What is the real name of the woman from Kicks Shoes?

   Talia: _____. Nick says her name is Jackie Baker, but she probably gave him a bogus name.

4. **Talia:** Where did Jackie go after lunch?

   Nick: _____. She left in a big hurry.

5. **Talia:** Why did Jackie want to meet you?

   Nick: _____ until I arrived at the Gower Building.

   She told me at the juice bar she had an interesting proposition for me, but she didn't tell me exactly what it was until the next day.

Grammar 3

Indefinite Pronouns

Talia has a problem with her credit card bill and has gone to a company office to ask about it. Fill in the blanks with an indefinite pronoun from the box. More than 1 answer may be correct, and you may use some pronouns more than once.

anyone	someone	everyone	no one	something	nothing
anybody	somebody	everybody	nobody	anything	everything

Receptionist: Can I help you with (1)___something___?

Talia: Yes, I'd like to speak with (2)_____ about my credit card bill.

Receptionist: And you haven't spoken to (3)_____ about the matter yet?

Talia: Actually, I have. Yesterday I spoke with Anna Nelson on the phone. She told me to come by today. She said she or (4)_____ else in the office could take care of (5)_____.

Receptionist: Anna? Anna Nelson? I don't think there's (6)_____ here by that name.

Talia: Oh, no! Not again! This is not my lucky day!

Language Functions

See Appendix 3 to review the language function charts.

Study Tip
Watch the characters' expressions and gestures in the video. Repeat what they say and try to imitate their expressions.

A. *Complete the conversations. Fill in each blank with 1 word to create an appropriate expression for expressing certainty or uncertainty and confirmation.*

1. **Amy:** I _____ that there'll be an Asian-American president of the United States in our lifetime.

   Talia: Really? I think there will be.

2. **Ryan:** I have _____ believing that humans really landed on the moon in 1969.

   Jeremy: I know. It is hard to believe, isn't it?

3. **John:** I _____ the world will run out of oil one day.

   Tony: I agree. No doubt about it.

4. **Jorge:** Do you really _____ it's worth exploring Mars?

   Ryan: Actually, I really doubt it.

5. **Amy:** Are you _____ that the Earth is getting hotter?

   Phil: Oh, yes. I'm sure about that. I've read all the research.

B. *Read the statements and questions from Exercise A again. Respond with your own opinion and add a comment.*

1. _Yes, no doubt about it. I think voters don't care about race anymore._

2. _____

3. _____

4. _____

5. _____

1. **Vocabulary.** Look up the words *say* and *talk* in a thesaurus. How many similar words can you find? For example, you will find words like *shout* ("say something loudly") and *chat* ("talk about a light topic"). Try to find at least 15 similar words. Make a diagram or map to show how the words are related.

2. **Listening and Grammar.** Keep a notebook. Write down examples of embedded questions that you hear. When you watch a movie or listen to the radio in English, listen for the ways that people ask questions. How many questions are "direct questions" (like *What is that?*) and how many questions are "embedded questions" (like *Can you tell me what this is?*).

3. **Writing.** What kinds of situations make you angry or frustrated—riding on a crowded train? being stuck in traffic? waiting in a long line? getting phone calls from sales people? Write 1 or 2 paragraphs explaining what makes you angry and how you deal with your anger or frustration in those situations.

4. **Speaking.** Think of 5 current situations involving national or international events. Make a list of "opinion statements," such as *(Name) will be elected this year.* Ask people if they agree or disagree with the statements. How certain are they?

5. **Project.** Research people's attitudes about work. Ask several people questions like these: *How do you feel about your work? What is the most satisfying part of your work? What is the most unsatisfying aspect of your work? What makes you happy at work? What makes you angry at work?* Consult websites or articles related to work. Give a short presentation to your class.

Grammar Explanations

This section contains the same grammar explanations that are found on the CD-ROM. They are included here for your quick reference. To view the animated presentation, go to the Grammar section of Unit B.4 in the CD-ROM course.

Grammar 1: *Used to*

1. We use *used to* + the base form of the verb to talk about **past habits** or **past situations** that are not true anymore.

   Receptionist: Jacob Banker used to work here.

   This means that Jacob Banker worked here in the past but doesn't work here anymore.

2. *Used to* always has a past meaning, but we only use it for something that happened regularly. We can't use it for something that happened only one time in the past. For one-time past events we use the **simple past tense**.

   Talia saw Nick yesterday.

   We do **NOT** say: ~~Talia used to see Nick yesterday.~~

3. To talk about things that did not happen regularly, *we can use the negative form **didn't use to**.*

   John didn't use to be a reporter. He was a researcher, like Talia.

   Notice that there is no -*d* at the end of *use*.

   We do **NOT** write: ~~didn't used to~~

   More often, we use *never* + *used to* instead.

   John never used to go to soccer games, but now he goes all the time.

4. To ask a question, we use *Did* + *use to*. Again, notice that there is no -*d* at the end of *use*.

   Did John use to like soccer when he was younger?

Grammar 2: Embedded *Wh-* Questions

1. An **embedded** question is a question that is inside another sentence.

   Receptionist: What are you talking about?
   I don't know what you're talking about.

   What you are talking about is an embedded question.

2. We often use **embedded** questions to ask politely for information.

   Talia: Excuse me. Can you tell me where the Gower Building is?

3. We start **embedded *wh-* questions** with a **question word**.

   Receptionist: I know who you want.
   Talia: Can you tell me where Jackie Baker works?
   Amy: Can you tell me how much this costs?

4. Notice that we use **statement word order**, not question word order, in embedded *wh-* questions.

   Talia: Where am I?
   I'm not sure where I am.

Notice, too, that we do not use *do*, *does*, or *did* in the embedded question.

   Receptionist: Who do you want?
   I know who you want.

Tony: What did you find out?
Can you tell me what you found out?

5. We can have an embedded question inside a statement or inside another question.

   When the embedded question is inside a statement, we put a period at the end of the sentence.
   I know what you want.

   When the **embedded question** is **inside a question**, we put a **question mark** at the end of the sentence.
   Can you tell me what you want?

Grammar 3: Indefinite Pronouns

1. We use **indefinite pronouns** when we are talking about people and things that we don't name. Sometimes we don't know exactly which person or thing we are talking about, and sometimes we don't want to name the person or thing yet.

   Receptionist: Someone is in big trouble.

   In the example, *someone* means a *person*. We can also use *somebody*. The meaning is the same.

2. We form indefinite pronouns with *some-*, *any-*, *no-*, and *every-*.

Indefinite Pronouns			
somebody	anybody	nobody	everybody
OR	OR	OR	OR
someone	anyone	no one	everyone
something	anything	nothing	everything

3. We use indefinite pronouns with *some-* in **affirmative** sentences.

   Something happened at the office today.
   Somebody brought in a tape.

   We also use indefinite pronouns with *some-* in **questions** when we think that the answer is *Yes*.

   Receptionist: Are you going to yell at somebody?
   Talia: Yes.

   In the example, the receptionist has a reason to think that Talia is going to yell.

   We also use indefinite pronouns with *some-* when we **make an offer** or **make a request.**

   Debbie: Would you like something to eat?
   Hans: No, thanks, but could I have something to drink?

4. We use indefinite pronouns with *any-* in **negative** statements.

> **Receptionist:** **There isn't anyone** here by that name.

> I **don't know anything** about soccer.

We also use indefinite pronouns with *any-* in **questions** when we don't know the answer.

> **Is there anyone** here named Jackie Baker?
> **Do you remember anything** about the game?

5. We use indefinite pronouns with *no* when the verb is **affirmative** but the meaning of the sentence is negative.

> **There is no one** in the office at the moment.

This sentence means the same as:

> **There isn't anyone** in the office at the moment.

Notice that we write *no one* as 2 words.

6. Indefinite pronouns always take **singular** verbs, even when they refer to more than 1 person or thing.

> There are **10 people** in my office, and **everybody loves** soccer.

In formal speech and writing we also use **singular** pronouns and possessive adjectives with indefinite pronouns.

> **Everybody** on the team knows what **he** has to do.
> **Everybody** knows **her** assignment.

When a group includes both males and females, we use *he* or *she* and *his* or *hers* in formal speech and writing.

> **Everyone** must hand in **his or her** test before leaving the classroom.

In conversation and informal writing, we usually use indefinite pronouns with *they* or *their*.

> **Everyone** in our class handed in **their** tests before leaving the classroom.

C.1 | No Help for Nick

🎧 **A. Listen to Track 25.** *Nick is talking to the receptionist at the Gower Building. Correct the mistakes in bold.*

Nick:	Jackie Baker, please.
Receptionist:	Oh, I'm sorry, but (1) **Jackie Baker isn't** here.
Nick:	Do you mind if I (2) **take a look** at that?
Receptionist:	Not at all. (3) **Go ahead**. . . . Let me guess. You're Nick.
Nick:	That's (4) **correct**, but . . . how did you know?
Receptionist:	Oh, you're famous!
Nick:	Oh. (5) **Are you a soccer fan?**
Receptionist:	Soccer? (6) **To tell the truth**, never watch it.

🎧 **B. Listen to Track 26.** *Nick and the receptionist continue talking. Complete this part of the conversation. There are 3 words in each blank.*

Receptionist:	So, Nick, is there anything else (1)_____ for you?
Nick:	Yeah, maybe. (2)_____ to someone else at Kicks?
Receptionist:	In fact, I've (3)_____ of them before today.
Nick:	I don't understand.
Receptionist:	Cheer up. Things can't be (4)_____ they seem.

🎧 **C. Listen to Track 27.** *Some models are being introduced at a fashion show. Fill in the missing adjectives. You will use some words more than once.*

beige	black	blue	colored	denim	gray	knees
long	oversized	plum	shoulder	sky	simple	

Michelle

_____-_____ shirt

_____ over-the-knee skirt

_____ _____ jacket

Liz

_____ cropped pants

_____-blue cardigan

_____, scooped-neck,

_____-sleeved sweater

_____ black tote

Shanika

_____ just-above-the-

_____ skirt

_____ _____ blouse

_____ _____ bag

Vocabulary

See Appendix 2 to review the vocabulary terms.

Here are some difficult situations for some people. What message can you give each person? Match the description of each person's situation with the best message. Sometimes more than one message is appropriate.

Situations

a **1.** Talia thinks she has solved the mystery, but she can't prove it yet.

____ **2.** Josh's friends are worried about him. His new girlfriend, Belinda, is always asking him for money.

____ **3.** Amy is angry because her friend borrowed her expensive jacket last week without asking. To make matters worse, she lost it!

____ **4.** Dean's girlfriend doesn't want to see him any more. Dean doesn't want to lose her.

____ **5.** Claire got a bad grade on her journalism test. Her friend doesn't think she should be so upset about it.

____ **6.** Jeremy is interested in covering a big news story. He's not a reporter yet, but he wants to try it.

____ **7.** Dean's girlfriend agrees to try the relationship again, but she wants to take it slowly. She doesn't want to make any big decisions about the relationship until later.

____ **8.** Tom is depressed. He interviewed for a new job but didn't get it.

____ **9.** Nick keeps telling everyone he didn't take the bribe. His family believes him, but a lot of other people don't.

Friend's Message

a. Hang in there! You can do it!

b. Lighten up! Things can't be as bad as you think!

c. Keep your cool. I know you're mad, but don't let our friendship melt away.

d. Have a heart! Give me 1 more chance!

e. Cheer up! I'm rooting for you!

f. Stick to your guns, even when the going gets rough!

g. Reach for your dreams! Go for it!

h. Watch out! The world can be a dangerous place. We don't want to see you get hurt!

i. Let's play it by ear and see what happens.

j. Life is full of unexpected things. Wait and see.

Grammar 1

Study Tip
List 3 of your grammar errors. Look them up in the CD-ROM Grammar Reference. Say the example sentences.

Past Continuous with *When*

Amy was a little "off" today. She kept doing things at the wrong time. Complete the sentences, using the past progressive or simple past of the verbs in parentheses. Add commas between the time clause and main clause when necessary. (Some sentences require simple past in both the main clause and the time clause.)

1. When Ms. Boyd (**fax**) _____was faxing_____ Amy's background research to the news office, she (**discover**) _____discovered_____ that there were several mistakes in Amy's research.

2. When the computer technician (**leave**) _____ the *Newsline* office, Amy (**realize**) _____ that she needed help with her computer. It was too late—the technician was gone.

3. When Amy's friend Liz (**walk**) _____ into the *Newsline* office for a surprise visit, Amy (**eat**) _____ lunch by herself at a nearby café. Unfortunately, they missed each other.

4. When Amy (**hear**) _____ that it was Jeremy's birthday, she (**buy**) _____ him a cake at a bakery. To Amy's surprise, when she (**return**) _____, all the employees at Newsline (**eat**) _____ cake. Talia had already bought one!

5. Talia (**watch**) _____ a movie with a friend when Amy (**call**) _____ her to ask her to dinner. Talia said, "Sorry, I can't. If only you had called me sooner!"

6. When Amy (**invite**) _____ Tom and Tina to come with her to dinner, they (**tell**) _____ her they had already eaten.

Grammar 2

Modals of Permission

Make requests for permission. Use the modals or phrases in parentheses. Then choose the appropriate response from the box below. More than 1 response may be appropriate.

No, not at all	No problem	Sure, go ahead	Fine with me
Be my guest	Help yourself	Yes, you can / may	Sorry, but . . .
I'd rather you didn't	No, I don't	Well, actually, yes, I do	

1. Talia wants to borrow Tony's book *Reporting 101: The Basics*. **(may)**

   Talia: ___May I borrow your book, Reporting 101: The Basics?___

   Tony: ___Help yourself___ . I have several other books on reporting if you're interested.

2. Amy wants to tape-record her grandmother's family stories. **(do you mind if)**

   Amy: _____

   Grandmother: _____. That's a lovely idea, dear.

3. Dean wants to use Nick's toothbrush. **(can)**

   Dean: _____

   Nick: _____. A towel is all right, but a toothbrush is too personal!

4. Roshawn wants to take Dean and his sister out to dinner. **(could)**

   Roshawn: _____

   Dean: _____. That would be great!

5. Ms. Boyd wants to work on a different story. **(may)**

   Ms. Boyd: _____

   Tony: _____. I really need you to do this one.

6. Tony's wife, Elisa, wants to send Talia a "hang in there" card. **(Is it OK if)**

   Elisa: _____

   Tony: _____. That might cheer her up.

BONUS
Write questions asking your teacher, another classmate, and a friend for permission to do something.

   EXAMPLE: (Teacher) ___May I meet with my study group in the classroom after class?___

1. (Teacher) _____

2. (Classmate) _____

3. (Friend) _____

Comparisons with *As* + Adjective + *As*

A. The members of Nick's soccer team have agreed to give Soccer World *magazine some information about their lives off the soccer field. Complete the sentences comparing teammates Dean and Roshawn. Use the information in the chart and the correct form of the words in parentheses.*

	Dean	Roshawn
Family	Has a brother and a sister	Has two sisters
Athletics	Plays soccer, football, and basketball; also snowboards	Plays soccer and tennis
Strength	Can lift 200 pounds	Can lift 150 pounds
Grades at university	Grade point average was 3.8 in college	Grade point average was 3.8 in college
Popularity	Receives over 100 fan letters a week	Receives about 5 fan letters a week

1. Dean's family ___is as big as Roshawn's family___. (**big**)
2. Roshawn ___isn't as athletic as Dean___. Dean ___is more athletic___. (**athletic**)
3. Dean _____. (**strong**)
4. Roshawn _____. (**lift weight**)
5. Roshawn's college grade point average _____. (**good**)
6. Roshawn _____. (**popular**)
7. Roshawn _____. (**receive fan letters**)

B. Now compare yourself to another person you know. You can use adjectives such as talented, energetic, *or* relaxed.

EXAMPLE: I'm not as energetic as my brother. He's more energetic than I am.

1. _____
2. _____

See Appendix 3 to review the language function charts.

A. Complete the conversations. Circle the correct word or phrase.

1. **Andrew:** Mom, I really don't want to go now. **Are / Do / Can** you mind if I don't go shopping with you?

   Elisa: Well, actually, yes, I **am / do / can**. I need you to help me carry stuff.

2. **Josh:** Is it OK **can / that / if** I use your computer for a while?

   Tom: **Go / Fine / Be** my guest.

3. **Andrew:** **OK / Mind / May** I leave class 10 minutes early today?

   Mr. Hanson: Well, I'd rather you **not / didn't / don't**. I'm giving out the test scores at the end of class.

4. **Amy:** **Let / Can / Maybe** me help you with those chairs.

   Claire: That's all right, but thanks **myself / anyway / you**.

5. **Elisa:** Do you need some **hand / hands / help** with choosing something to wear?

   Andrew: Sure, **help yourself / I'd appreciate it / I can do it myself**.

B. Write conversations for the given situations. Use expressions for offering help, accepting or declining help, asking for permission, and giving or refusing permission.

1. You see your classmate is having problems with an exercise. She wants your help.

   You (*offer to help*): _____Here, let me help you._____

   Your classmate (*accepts your help*): _____That's nice of you._____

2. You are saving seats for your friends in the movie theater. A couple wants to sit there.

   Couple (*ask permission to sit there*): _____

   You (*refuse, give a reason*): _____

3. You're sitting on the train. You have finished with your newspaper. Someone wants to read it.

   Other person (*ask for permission*): _____

   You (*give permission*): _____

4. You're standing next to your car on the street. Someone stops to ask if you need help.

   Other person (*offer to help*): _____

   You (*decline their help, give a reason*): _____

Application Activities

1. **Grammar.** Find several photographs, or pictures from a magazine, with at least 4 or 5 people in them. Say several statements about them using the past progressive with *when*; for example, *When Joe was eating, Harry was cleaning up.*

2. **Vocabulary and Listening.** Listen to an advice show on the radio or TV or find an advice site on the Internet. Listen or look for idiomatic phrases that the helper uses to give advice (for example, *Don't bite off more than you can chew*). Try to list at least 5 phrases.

3. **Writing.** Think of someone you know well. Describe the appearance and personality of this person. Compare him or her to yourself. Use comparative adjectives and phrases.

4. **Presentation.** Put on an advice show for your class. In advance, collect a "problem card" from each student in the class. Each student will write a problem but leave off his or her name. The problem can be real or imagined. In a group of 3 or 4, read through the problems. Select 3 interesting problems and prepare at least 2 specific pieces of advice for the person. Present your advice to the class.

5. **Project.** Find a website that specializes in greeting cards. Some cards are to congratulate people, some are to cheer people up, and so on. Write down, or print out, the greetings from at least 3 cards. Compare them with those your classmates found. Which are the most popular greeting cards?

Grammar Explanations

This section contains the same grammar explanations that are found on the CD-ROM. They are included here for your quick reference. To view the animated presentation, go to the Grammar section of Unit C.1 in the CD-ROM course.

Grammar 1: Past Continuous with *When*

1. We use the **past continuous** with ***when*** to talk about an activity that was already in progress when something else happened. Notice that we use the **simple past** after ***when***.

   Receptionist: I was getting ready to leave when you arrived.

   This means that the receptionist started getting ready **before** the visitor arrived.

2. The **time clause** (the part of the sentence with ***when***) can come at the **beginning or end of the sentence**. When the time clause comes at the beginning of the sentence, we need a comma after the time clause.

   I was getting ready to leave. You arrived.

   When you arrived, I was getting ready to leave.

   When the time clause comes at the end of the sentence, there is no comma.

   I was getting ready to leave **when you arrived**.

   Notice that the meaning doesn't change when you change the order of the 2 parts of the sentence. The 2 sentences both mean that the receptionist started getting ready to leave before the visitor arrived.

3. Notice the difference in meaning between these 2 sentences:

   When the phone rang, the receptionist was leaving.

   This means that first the receptionist started to leave and then the phone rang. We use the past continuous to show that 1 action **was already in progress** when the other action happened.

   When the phone rang, the receptionist left.

   This means that first the phone rang, and then the receptionist left. We use the simple past in both clauses to show that one action happened **after** the other action.

Grammar 2: Modals of Permission

1. We use ***may***, ***could***, and ***can*** plus a subject and the base form of the verb to ask for **permission**.

   Nick: May I speak to someone at Kicks?
   Could I speak to someone at Kicks?
   Can I speak to someone at Kicks?

   May is more formal than *could* and *can*. *Can* is the least formal.

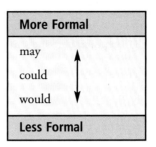

2. We often use ***please*** to ask for permission more **politely**.

   Please can go before the base form of the verb.
   Nick: May I speak to someone at Kicks?
   May I please speak to someone at Kicks?

   Please can also go at the end of the question. When this happens, we use a comma before *please*.
   Nick: May I speak to someone at Kicks, please?

3. We usually **answer** questions about permission with words like ***yes***, ***sure***, ***certainly***, ***of course***, and ***go ahead***.
   Nick: Could I ask you a question?
   Receptionist: Sure.

   We can use ***may*** or ***can*** in short answers about permission, but we never use *could*.
   Nick: Could I look at the directory?
   Receptionist: Yes, of course you can.

   We do **NOT** say: ~~Yes, you could.~~

4. We can also use ***Do you mind*** to ask **permission**. Expressions with *Do you mind* are followed by ***if*** plus a sentence.
   Nick: Do you mind if I look at that?

   Do you mind is very polite. We do not use *please* with *Do you mind*.

5. We answer *Do you mind* questions with ***Not at all***.
   Nick: Do you mind if I look at that?
   Receptionist: Not at all. Have a look.

   Not at all means *It's OK. You can do it.* If you answer *Yes* to a question with *Do you mind*, you mean *It's not OK. You can't do it.*

   We can also answer a *Do you mind* question with *Sure* or *Go ahead*.

6. When we say *No* to a question about permission, we usually **apologize** and **give a reason**.
   Nick: May I speak to someone else at Kicks?
   Receptionist: Sorry, Nick, but there's no Kicks here, either.

Grammar 3: Comparisons with *As* + Adjective + *As*

1. Sometimes we want to talk about ways 2 people or things are **the same**. To talk about a similarity, we use *as* + **adjective** + *as*.

    Receptionist: Maybe you can describe Jackie Baker.
    Nick: She's **as tall as** you are.

    Nick means that Jackie and the receptionist are the same height.

2. Sometimes we want to talk about ways 2 people or things are **different**. To talk about a difference, we use *not as* + **adjective** + *as*.

    Things are**n't as bad as** they seem.

3. When the meaning is clear, we often leave out the second part of the comparison.

    Bea: Dean's a good player, but is he as good as Nick?
    Zach: Sure. He's just **as good**.

    In this example, Zach means Dean is *as good as Nick*.

C.2 | In the News

🎧 **A. Listen to Track 28.** *Nick is talking to Patty, the juice bar attendant at the health club, while the TV news is on. Complete this part of the conversation.*

Patty: What can I get (1)_____ you?

Nick: Could I get a large pineapple and strawberry smoothie?

Patty: Coming right (2)_____. Is everything all right?

Nick: My life is a mess! And just when I thought things were going great.

Patty: What's the matter? Did you get hurt?

Nick: Yeah, I got hurt. But not (3)_____ the soccer field.
***
Hold (4)_____. Do you see that woman? The one standing (5)_____

Dean? . . . I think that's Jackie Baker! The woman (6)_____ Kicks Shoes.

🎧 **B. Listen to Track 29.** *Patty is telling Nick about Jackie. Complete this part of the conversation. There are 3 words in each blank.*

Patty: Jackie Baker? No. That's Jackie Bishop, Dean's sister. She was a member here last year,

but I haven't (1)_____ lately. I'm surprised you never

(2)_____.
***
Oh yeah! She's (3)_____ a lot of movie parts, but I doubt she's ever actually acted in anything.

Nick: Except for the day she (4)_____ lunch. She's a great actress.

(5)_____ an Oscar for her performance.

🎧 **C. Listen to Track 30.** *You will hear 2 recipes. Complete the list of ingredients for each one.*

Summer Sling smoothie

   3 peeled bananas_____
___ sliced_____
2 ____ of vanilla _____
___ cup of crushed _____

Avocado Dream sandwich

   2 slices of whole grain bread____
___ slices of Swiss _____
_____ of avocado
_____ tomato
4 slices of _____
1 tablespoon of _____

Vocabulary

See Appendix 2 to review the vocabulary terms.

Talia is at her health club, Sleek Physique, for her weekly exercise. Complete the sentences with the correct phrasal verb from the box. Be sure to use the correct form and tense.

break down	catch up on	come up with	fall for	go ahead
try out	hold on	look into	look up to	run into

Conversation 1

Talia: Natalie! I didn't expect to (1)_____run into_____ you! I never get a chance to see you!

Natalie: Talia! Great to see you! We can finally (2)_____ things! I want to know what's going on in your life.

Talia: Oh! That's my cell phone. (3)_____, Natalie.

Talia: (*on the phone*) OK, Tony, I'll do it first thing in the morning. Bye.

Talia: Sorry, Natalie. (4)_____. What were you saying?

Natalie: So, Talia, tell me—I've been hearing about you and some guy. Have you actually

(5)_____ someone new?

Talia: Me? In love? Right now? That's ridiculous. Somebody's telling you stories!

Conversation 2

Talia: Ugh! This exercise bike is always (6)_____! Can't they fix these things?!

Pete: I know. That one always has something wrong. The manager told me he's going to

(7)_____ it. He's not sure what the problem is. You know, Talia, you can

go pretty fast on that exercise bike. Have you thought about (8)_____

for Sleek Physique's bicycling team?

Talia: Oh, stop, Pete! You're embarrassing me!

Conversation 3

Talia: Where's Rosa? She's supposed to be here for our 6:00 p.m. aerobics class.

Yolanda: I don't know. She told me she would be here, but she always (9)_____

a good excuse.

Talia: I'm really disappointed in her. Everyone in the class made a promise to be here and

encourage each other.

Yolanda: Well, why don't you call her right now? She'll listen to you; she really

(10)_____ you, you know. She thinks you're really smart and cool.

Inseparable Phrasal Verbs

Talia, Amy, and Claire are talking about their favorite soap opera, One Heart to Give. *Complete the sentences, using 3-part phrasal verbs. Use the preposition only when appropriate.*

catch up (on) = learn
drop out (of) = quit
end up (with) = have at the end
give in (to) = agree to after much persuasion
go along (with) = follow
is going on (with) = is happening
show up (for) = arrive
turn out (for) = end up
work out (for) = conclude well

Talia: So what (1)_____'s going on with_____ Kristen and Leland?

Amy: You haven't had much time to (2)_____ the story, have you?

Claire: Shhhh! Here comes a commercial for *One Heart to Give*. Maybe it'll tell us something.

TV announcer: Will Kristen (3)_____ the handsome and charming Leland Castle?

Will their wedding day be as perfect as they dreamed . . . or will Penelope

(4)_____ and steal him away?

Will things (5)_____ Brandon Hunkstrom? Can Delilah convince him to

(6)_____ her evil plans? Will he (7)_____?

Will Mrs. Richford's daughter, Stephanie, remember her dreams of finishing medical school?

Or will she (8)_____ and run away with Brent?

How will things (9)_____ our friends? Tune in to *One Heart to Give* this Friday to find out!

Talia: Aww! They never tell us anything! I guess we'll have to wait and see.

Gerunds and Infinitives

Jeremy works at Newsline. *He and his wife are expecting their first baby. The* Newsline *staff members are giving him suggestions for a name. Complete the sentences with the gerund or infinitive form of the verbs in parentheses.*

1. **Jeremy:** My wife and I still need (**find**) _____to find_____ a good name for our baby. Would

   you guys mind (**help**) _____helping_____ us out?

2. **Jeremy:** We're expecting him or her (**arrive**) _____ sometime within the next

   2 weeks.

3. **Claire:** You mean you don't know if it's a boy or a girl?

   Jeremy: No. We wanted (**wait**) _____ (**find out**) _____.

4. **Ryan:** If it's a boy, how about Winston? Or Wesley?

   Jeremy: Cynthia and I agreed (**not pick**) _____ a name that the other one didn't

   like. I think Wesley is on her "no" list.

5. **Talia:** Have you considered (**choose**) _____ something really different?

   How about Kiah? It's an Australian aboriginal name; it means "from a beautiful place."

6. **Jeremy:** Not a bad idea. We're both American, but we've decided (**not let**) _____

   that stop us from (**look into**) _____ names from other cultures.

7. **Amy:** I know! If it's a girl, how about (**name**) _____ her after a food or spice like

   Honey or Ginger . . . or Cinnamon?

8. **Jeremy:** I don't know . . . but thanks, everybody. Um, I think Cynthia and I will keep (**look**)

   _____ . . .

   Tad: Nemo!?

   Amy: Fifi!?

   Jeremy: . . . by ourselves!!

BONUS
What would you name your child? Use verb + verb combinations, with want, prefer, would like,
enjoy, *or* avoid.

> *EXAMPLES:* I would prefer to name my baby Rose. I think it's a beautiful name.
>
> I would avoid naming a baby Young. There are too many people in my culture with that name.

1. _____

2. _____

Grammar 3

Future Time Clauses

A. *Fortune cookies contain a message, usually a prediction for the future. Read these fortunes. Decide which sentence should become a main clause and which sentence should become the time clause. (The most important information goes in the main clause.) Then combine the sentences into 1 sentence, adding a comma where necessary.*

1. You'll finish an important job. You won't find love before that.

   _____ You won't find love _____ **until** _____ you finish an important job. _____ .

2. Something big will happen to you. Then the month will end.

   Before the month _____ , something big _____ to you.

3. You will listen and ask questions. Then you will know the truth.

   After _____ .

4. You will learn who you can trust. Then your life will be richer.

   _____ **as soon as** _____ .

5. Your friends will say many things about you. At that time, you will be away.

   _____ **while** _____ .

6. Your troubles will be over. Then you will receive many rewards.

   As soon as _____ .

7. You will help a friend. He or she will need you.

   _____ **just when** _____ .

8. You will face the truth. You won't succeed before that.

   Until _____ .

9. Someone will impress you. You won't expect it.

   _____ **when** _____ .

10. You will receive some surprising news. Then you will make an important decision.

    Just before _____ .

B. *What would you like to see written on* your *fortune? Use time clauses.*

EXAMPLE: As soon as you finish this English program, you will speak English very well.

1. _____

2. _____

Language Functions

See Appendix 3 to review the language function charts.

A. *Some people at* Newsline *are discussing current issues. Replace each boldfaced phrase with a similar phrase. Use the phrases in the box below, or use other expressions for asking for and giving opinions.*

do you believe	I'm not really sure	If you ask me
To tell the truth	What are your feelings about	What do you think of

                  What do you think of

Talia: (1) ~~What's your opinion about~~ the new smoking regulation?

Josh: (2) **In my opinion**, it's time that we go ahead with it. I don't think people should smoke in office buildings. Anywhere. Anytime. Period.

Andy: So tell me, Tony, (3) **do you think** Mega Communications will take over *Newsline*?

Tony: You know, (4) **I really can't say**. I think we just have to wait and see.

Amy: (5) **What do you make of** the new "Friday Fashion" idea?

Ms. Boyd: (6) **Frankly**, I don't know how they came up with this idea. I prefer to wear professional clothes at work every day!

B. *Write your own conversation about a current topic.*

Your friend: _____

You: _____

Application Activities

Study Tip
As you watch the CD-ROM video, list words and phrases that are difficult to pronounce. Repeat these words every day.

1. **Grammar/Vocabulary.** Make index cards with phrasal verbs. Try to find at least 20 phrasal verbs. Use your dictionary to discover new phrasal verbs, or skim through the advertisements in magazines and newspapers. Look up verbs such as these: *go, get, give, take, bring, turn.* Write sample sentences for each verb. Divide the cards into 2-word and 3-word phrasal verbs.

2. **Writing.** What news programs are popular now? Why are they popular? Take a brief survey. Ask at least 4 people about their favorite news programs and their favorite news announcers. Write a report about your results.

3. **Speaking.** Choose 2 current topics related to international politics or sports. Consult this week's newspapers or current news websites. Discuss your opinions. Use the expressions for asking for opinions and giving opinions from the Language Functions, Appendix 3.

4. **Project.** Did you know that Nick means "victory of the people" and Talia means "blossoming flower" (Greek)? Use the Internet to find out the meaning and place/language origin of your teacher's name, your classmates' names, or any other names you are curious about.

Grammar Explanations

This section contains the same grammar explanations that are found on the CD-ROM. They are included here for your quick reference. To view the animated presentation, go to the Grammar section of Unit C.2 in the CD-ROM course.

Grammar 1: Inseparable Phrasal Verbs

1. **Phrasal verbs** are verbs that have 2 parts—a **verb** + a **particle**.

   > **Run into** is a phrasal verb.

   > *Run* is the verb; *into* is the particle.

   The particle looks just like a preposition, but it is actually 1 part of this 2-part verb. The particle often changes the meaning of the verb.

   > **Patty:** I'm surprised you never **ran into** her.

   In the example, *ran into* means *met by chance*. As you can see, the verb *run* plus the particle *into* has a completely different meaning from the verb *run* by itself.

2. Some phrasal verbs are **inseparable**. This means that the 2 parts—verb and particle—always stay together. When an inseparable phrasal verb has an object, the object always comes after the 2 parts of the verb.

   > **Reporter:** What do you **think of this scandal**?
   > **Dean:** I'm not sure what I **think of it**. I don't have enough information.

   In the conversation, the noun *this scandal* and the pronoun *it* are objects of the verb *think of*. Both noun and pronoun objects always come **after** an inseparable phrasal verb.

   We do **NOT** say: ~~I'm not sure what I think it of.~~

3. Some phrasal verbs are used with **certain prepositions** when they have an object. We sometimes call these combinations **3-part verbs**; 3-part verbs are inseparable.

   > **Nick:** I need to **catch up on** the news.

   The phrasal verb *catch up* means *do something you did not have time to do before*. We use it with the preposition *on* when there is an object.

   We don't use the preposition when there is no object.

   > **Nick:** I've been so busy. I need some time to **catch up**.

Grammar 2: Gerunds and Infinitives

1. The **gerund** is the **base form** of the verb + *-ing*.
   > **playing**

2. The **infinitive** is *to* + the **base form** of the verb.
   > **to play**

3. Some verbs can be followed by the **gerund**.
   > **Nick:** Would you **mind making** it louder?
   > **Dean:** He wouldn't **risk ruining** his career.
   > **Patty:** She **keeps changing** her hair color.

   We form the **negative** by using *not* before the gerund.
   > Would you mind repeating that?
   > Would you **mind not repeating** that?

Some verbs that can be followed by the gerund		
avoid	consider	enjoy
finish	keep	mind
miss	practice	prefer
quit	risk	stop

4. Some verbs can be followed by the **infinitive**.
   > **Nick:** I **agreed to endorse** some shoes.
   > I **need to catch up on** the news.

   We form the **negative** by using *not* before the infinitive.
   > I decided to go to the game.
   > I **decided not to go** to the game.

Some verbs that can be followed by the infinitive		
agree	begin	decide
expect	hope	learn
need	prefer	seem
wait	want	would like

Grammar 3: Future Time Clauses

1. **Future time clauses** begin with time words like *when*, *after*, *before*, *as soon as*, *until*, and *while*. We use future time clauses with main clauses to talk about what is going to happen in the future.

   > **Dean:** I'm sure they'll decide **as soon as they have more information**.

   In the example, *I'm sure they'll decide* is the **main clause**. *As soon as they have more information* is the future time clause.

   Future time clauses talk about the future but they **use the present**.

   > **Dean:** I'm not going to comment **until we know more**.

   We do **NOT** say: ~~until we will know more~~

   The main clause **uses the future**—with *will* or *be going to*.

   > **Dean:** I'm not **going to** comment until we know more.

2. The **future time clause** can come at the **beginning or the end** of the sentence. The meaning does not change. When the future time clause comes at the beginning of the sentence, we use a **comma** after it.

   > **Nick:** **When I get home**, I'll watch TV.
   > I'll watch TV **when I get home**.

C.3 The Truth Revealed

Listening

🎧 **A. Listen to Track 31.** *Talia and Amy are talking about the Nick Crawford story. Complete this part of the conversation.*

Talia: I'm so glad I went to that class last night. It was really (1)_____.

Amy: Well, Talia, you do look a little (2)_____ today.

Talia: Well, I don't feel (3)_____ better.

Amy: You know what? You missed a (4)_____ party the other night. Josh's friend, Matt, was there. I really want to introduce you to him. He's . . .

Talia: I completely believed him. He can be so (5)_____. So convincing. I am so (6)_____. I feel like such a fool.

Amy: Look, Talia, you're no fool. Don't be so (7)_____ on yourself.

Talia: But I was (8)_____ that Nick was being (9)_____.

🎧 **B. Listen to Track 32.** *Nick is explaining to Talia what happened with Jackie Baker. Complete this part of the conversation with the correct form of the verbs in parentheses.*

Talia: I'll (1) **(give)** _____ you 2 minutes.

Nick: You (2) **(not be)** _____ sorry. OK, I (3) **(go)** _____ to see her. I (4) **(go)** _____ to (5) **(see)** _____ Jackie Baker.

Talia: There is no Jackie Baker.

Nick: That's right.

Talia: So you admit that you (6) **(lie)** _____?

Nick: No, I (7) **(not lie)** _____. No, listen, this is what happened. . . . She (8) **(trick)** _____ me. She and her brother Dean. They (9) **(want)** _____ me out of the way. Dean is next in line to be the star player.

Talia: Wow! This is amazing. So, what (10) **(you do)** _____ now?

Nick: I'll (11) **(go)** _____ to the team office to talk to the coach. I've got to make sure he believes me.

🎧 **C. Listen to Track 33.** *You will hear a news story about a soccer player's contract. Correct the errors in the sentences.*

1. Gomez is now signed through the ~~2008~~ *2007* season.

2. Gomez's annual salary will be $5.4 million.

3. Gomez said she will receive a bonus of $1.5 million each year that the Orbits are in first or second place.

4. Gomez will receive 2.5 percent of the Orbits ticket sales for home games and 1.5 percent of sales of Orbit sweaters with her number, zero-zero.

5. Gomez agrees to appear in 2 new Orbits Shoes TV commercials.

6. Gomez will not appear in any other promotional material for the team.

Vocabulary

See Appendix 2 to review the vocabulary terms.

Amy and Claire are planning a party. Complete the conversations with the appropriate idiomatic expressions in the box.

out of control	out of date	out of it	out of place	out of sorts
out of work	out of the blue	out of the question	out of the way	out of this world

1. **Claire:** What's wrong, Amy? You seem

   _____*out of it*_____ today. Are you getting enough sleep?

   Amy: Oh, I'm fine, just really tired.

2. **Amy:** You know, I'd love to have a party here in the apartment.

   Claire: That's a great idea. But it's a little

   _____.

   Amy: I know. I guess I've been feeling _____ because of all the work at the office. But I want to have fun this Friday.

3. **Claire:** Last time we had a party, it got _____. Remember—a couple of guys were jumping off the roof into the swimming pool!

   Amy: Yes, I remember! *This* time jumping off the roof is _____! Our landlord says if one more party gets out of hand, I'm out of here!

4. Claire: Well, let's start planning. Who should we invite?

   Amy: We've got to invite Andy Nomura to the party this time. He's been

   _____ since his company went out of business last month, and he's

   depressed. Maybe the party will help him feel better.

5. Amy: A lot of the guests won't know each other, so we'd better plan some get-to-know-you

   games. I don't want anyone to feel _____.

6. Claire: Good thinking. Let's see. What else? Ah! We'll need a place to dance.

   Amy: I think we'll have enough room for dancing if we move the furniture

   _____.

7. Claire: Don't forget the music!

   Amy: I think we need to buy some new CDs. Our music collection is _____.

   No one wants to listen to 1980s music any more.

8. Claire: Wait! I think 1980s music would be perfect for the party! Let's ask everyone to come

   dressed in 80s clothes.

   Amy: Then I guess I'd better look in the back of my closet for my old parachute pants! This

   party's going to be _____!

Grammar 1

Infinitives of Purpose

A. Write short answers to the questions using an infinitive of purpose. Use your imagination.

1. Why did Talia go <u>s</u>hopping at the department store

   last week?   <u>To buy a gift for her friend</u>

2. Why did <u>A</u>my call Talia last night?   _____

3. Why did Josh turn on the tele<u>v</u>ision?   _____

4. Why did Clair<u>e</u> take the bus?   _____

5. Why d<u>i</u>d Tony go to France?   _____

6. Why was Talia hurrying <u>M</u>onday at <u>e</u>xactly 8:00 a.m.? _____

BONUS

Write all the <u>underlined</u> letters in the Exercise A questions in the blanks below. Keep the same order. The result will be the answer to the riddle. Do you understand it?

Riddle: Why did Talia give her watch to the bank?

Answer: To __ __ __ __ __ __ __ __!

B. *Choose 2 actions that you did recently from the list below. Write complete sentences telling the purpose of those activities.*

move to (place)	change jobs	go to (name of a store)
go (city)	call (name of someone)	

EXAMPLES: Five years ago, I moved to Dallas to be near my parents.

Last night, I went to the grocery store to buy some milk and vegetables.

1. _____

2. _____

Grammar 2

Modals of Necessity

A. *Nick's friend Katy Golden is a star soccer player on the women's national team. She is considering signing a contract with You Go Girl! sports clothing. Her agent is telling her about the contract. Circle the correct form of the verb in each sentence.*

1. You can't **doing / do** commercials or advertisements for other clothing or shoe companies during the 1-year contract.

2. You **have / 've** to wear You Go Girl! fashions for at least 75% of your games and for 100% of your television interviews.

3. You can wear other clothing, but the brand name **must not / doesn't have to** be visible. You Go Girl! doesn't want your fans to see the name of another company.

4. You **'ve got / must** to do at least 3 commercials and 3 print ads for You Go Girl!

5. There will be 6 company events. You **don't have / doesn't have** to attend more than half of these events.

6. You Go Girl! **must / has** to provide you with a different outfit for every television interview. You **doesn't / don't** have to return the outfits to the company.

7. If you are involved in a scandal, You Go Girl **doesn't have / hasn't** to wait until the end of the contract. It may end the contract immediately if it believes the scandal will hurt the company.

8. This happened to Jen Starr. Last year, Ms. Starr was accused of stealing some jewelry from a department store. You Go Girl! **had / has** to end Jen's contract early to protect itself.

9. You're going to **have to / must** think about this contract carefully before deciding.

B. *Based on the information in Exercise A, decide whether the sentences are true (T) or false (F).*

  _T_   **1.** Katy may do ads for Fender Blender, the smoothie company, during her 1 year contract with You Go Girl!, but she may not do ads for Step on It!, the athletic footwear company.

  _____   **2.** Katy must wear only You Go Girl! fashions.

  _____   **3.** If Katy wears a sweatshirt with the name of another company across it during a soccer game, You Go Girl! might end the contract with her.

  _____   **4.** Katy can attend more than 3 company events if she wants to.

  _____   **5.** If Katy is involved in a scandal, You Go Girl! cannot end the contract until the 1 year is finished.

Grammar 3

Participial Adjectives

A. *Complete the sentences with the adjectives that best describe each situation. Choose a verb from the box and add the correct participial ending (-ed or -ing) to make it into an adjective.*

exhaust	bore	amuse (entertain)	disgust	confuse
frustrate	disappoint	surprise	shock	interest

1. Talia told some funny stories at the party. The guests laughed all night long.
   Talia was ___amusing___. The guests were ___amused___.

2. The soccer team didn't play very well today; they didn't score even 1 goal. Everyone felt really bad about it. The players and fans were _____. The game was _____.

3. Soccer practice was difficult today. Coach Haskins made the team run a few extra miles. Then he made the team practice on the field for 3 extra hours. The practice was _____. The _____ players couldn't wait until it was over.

4. There was a guest speaker in last week's journalism class. Mr. Manzoni gave a very long, serious speech about reporting. Some students fell asleep. The journalism students were not at all _____. In fact, they were really _____. The guest speaker was so _____.

5. Mr. Manzoni's lesson was also hard to understand. He couldn't make his idea clear. The students were completely _____ by the lecture. It was very _____.

6. Jen Starr, the famous female soccer player, was interviewed on TV today. Suddenly, she became very angry and started shouting. No one could believe it! Jen's behavior was very _____. The fans were _____.

7. Jen said some terrible things about the league's soccer officials. She used a lot of bad words. Many people thought Jen's language was _____. They were _____ by it.

B. *Write sentences about yourself. Use the participial adjectives from Exercise A.*

EXAMPLE: Lord of the Rings was entertaining. I was entertained because of the great special effects.

1. _____

2. _____

3. _____

Language Functions

See Appendix 3 to review the language function charts.

Rearrange the words to make conversations.

1. **Tony:**   anything / Do / me / you / to / need / do

   _____?

   Elisa: really / I / you / to / with / need / Yes / me / this / help

   _____.

2. **Talia:**   to / work / essential / finish / me / for / It's / this / today

   _____.

   Amy: do / me / What / do / you / to / need

   _____?

3. **Coach Haskins's assistant:**   do / you / need / to / me / Is / anything / there

   _____?

   Coach Haskins: I / It's / these / important / to / send / documents / that / really / *Newsline*

   _____.

4. **Talia:**   think / idea / I've / of / good / really / got / a / to

   _____.

   Claire: help / to / me / to / something / you / Do / do / need

   _____?

Application Activities

Study Tip
Find a study partner. Choose 3 dialogs from the exercises in this book and act them out. Use appropriate gestures!

1. **Grammar.** Make a list of participial adjectives. Divide the list into 2 columns, one for those ending in *-ed,* the other for those ending in *-ing.* For each pair of adjectives, write two sentences to illustrate the meaning. For example, *My brother is amazing. I am amazed by my brother.*

2. **Vocabulary.** Collect expressions and idioms beginning with prepositions (*in, on, under, out of, through*), like *out of this world.* Start with these (use your dictionary to check meaning): *in touch/over a barrel/up in arms/under the weather/down and out/through and through/at a loss.* Use each expression in a sentence.

3. **Writing.** Write about a time you negotiated with someone. It could be a parent, a friend, a business client, or someone else. What did you want? What did the other person want? What did you do? What was the result?

4. **Speaking.** Talk to someone about his or her plans in life. What things will make that person happy (or unhappy) if they don't have them? Think about relationships, money, possessions, where they live, the state of the world. Use expressions of purpose, such as *Do you (study English) to (get a better job)?*

5. **Project.** Use the Internet, TV, billboards, and magazines to find 5 famous people who endorse products. Why do you think the companies involved wanted these people? Do you think product endorsement by other people makes a difference in what you buy or to people in general? Should famous people advertise things that are outside of their own profession? Discuss your findings and your opinions with your class.

Grammar Explanations

This section contains the same grammar explanations that are found on the CD-ROM. They are included here for your quick reference. To view the animated presentation, go to the Grammar section of Unit C.3 in the CD-ROM course.

Grammar 1: Infinitives of Purpose

1. We use **infinitives of purpose** to give the **reason** for something. They answer the question *Why?*
   John: Why is Nick Crawford here?
   Amy: He's here **to talk** with Talia.

   In the example, the infinitive (*to* plus the base form of the verb) explains why Nick is here.

2. In conversation, you can answer *Why* questions with the infinitive of purpose. You can give long or short answers.
   Talia: Why did you go to the Gower Building?
   Nick: I went there **to see** Jackie Baker.
   To see Jackie Baker.

3. We sometimes use the longer form **in order to** plus the base form of the verb to give reasons. This form is more formal.
   The Soccer Federation is investigating Nick Crawford **in order to determine** if he accepted a bribe.

4. To talk about a **negative purpose**, use **in order not to** plus the base form of the verb.
   Jackie took Nick out to lunch **in order not to reveal** that she didn't have an office.

Grammar 2: Modals of Necessity

1. We use **have to** plus the base form of the verb to talk about **necessity**—things people need to do.
   Nick: I **have to leave**.

   Notice that there is no contraction for *have to*.

   We do **NOT** say: ~~I've to leave.~~

   We also use **have got to** plus the base form of the verb to talk about necessity. *Have got to* often expresses **strong feelings**.
   Nick: I'm going to talk to the coach. I**'ve got to make sure** he believes me.

   We usually use the contraction for *have got to*.
   Nick: I have got to speak to Talia.
   I**'ve** got to speak to Talia.

2. We can also use **must** plus the base form of the verb to talk about necessity. *Must* is stronger than *have to* and *have got to*.
   Nick: I **must prove** that I'm innocent!

   We often use *must* to write or talk about rules.
   Athletes **must wear** special shoes for running.

3. We use **don't have to** or **doesn't have to** to talk about things that are **not necessary** to do.
   Nick: I **don't have to speak** to you. I'll give my story to that other reporter.

   This means that it isn't necessary for Nick to speak to Talia. He has another choice.

4. We use **must not** or **cannot** to talk about things that are **prohibited**. This means that they are **not allowed**. They are against the rules or against the law.
   Athletes **must not accept** bribes. It's against the law. This means that athletes *can't* accept bribes.

   We do not usually use contractions for *must not*, but we often use the contraction *can't* for *cannot*.

5. When we **ask** questions about necessity, we usually use **have to**. We don't usually use *must* or *have got to*.
   Does Talia **have to work** late tonight?

6. We use *must* and *have got to* only for **present** and **future** necessity. For **all other tenses** and forms we use a form of **have to**.
   Talia **has had to** work late every night this week. (present perfect)
   She **had to** work late last week, too. (simple past)
   She **doesn't want to have to** work late again. (after infinitive with *to*)

Grammar 3: Participial Adjectives

1. **Participial adjectives** end in **-ed** and **-ing**. They usually describe feelings or reactions.

Participial Adjectives	
amaz**ed**	amaz**ing**
depress**ed**	depress**ing**
surpris**ed**	surpris**ing**

2. We use **-ed adjectives** to talk about how someone **feels**.
   Talia: I am so **disappointed**.
   Oh, I'm so **depressed**.

3. We use **-ing adjectives** to talk about someone or something that **causes a feeling or reaction**.
   Talia: I went to class last night. It was really **interesting**.

   In the example, the class was *interesting*. As a result, Talia was *interested*.
   Talia: This is **amazing**.

   In the example, Talia is talking about Nick's story. The story is *amazing*. As a result, it makes her feel *amazed*.

C.4 Dean's Challenge

Listening

🎧 **A. Listen to Track 34.** *Nick is talking to Coach Haskins. Complete this part of the conversation. Use a form of the verb in parentheses.*

Nick: Oh, good, you're here. Coach, I

(1) **(try)** _____'ve been trying_____ to speak

to you since last night. This whole scandal . . .

Coach: Nick, we (2) **(work)** _____

together for 4 years now. You're my best player,

and frankly, Nick, I feel like we're family.

Nick: Thanks, Coach. Me, too.

Coach: I'm sorry. I didn't know you (3) **(have)** _____ money problems.

Nick: No, I haven't! I hope you don't believe those lies about me. Trust me, Coach, I

(4) **(let down)** _____ you _____.

🎧 **B. Listen to Track 35.** *Nick is confronting Dean. Match the beginnings and endings of the sentences.*

_j_	1. Tough rap	a.	expect me to figure it out.
___	2. Is there anything	b.	what you're talking about.
___	3. You can tell Coach	c.	you pulled it off.
___	4. What are you	d.	that fake endorsement deal.
___	5. I don't know	e.	you were that smart.
___	6. The two of you dreamed up	f.	I can do to help?
___	7. I didn't know	g.	talking about?
___	8. I guess you didn't	h.	what really happened.
___	9. It's one of the craziest	i.	stories I've ever heard.
___	10. I don't know how	j.	you're taking.

🎧 **C. Listen to Track 36.** *You will hear a presentation about the 4 principles of coaching. Read each statement below. If it's consistent with (similar to) this coach's philosophy, write C. If it's not consistent with (different from) his philosophy, write NC.*

_C_ **1.** You have to be committed to excellence.

_____ **2.** You should always try to improve.

_____ **3.** You need to let failure teach you.

_____ **4.** You must realize that success has a high price.

_____ **5.** Your personal achievement is more important than the team's achievement.

_____ **6.** It's important to want to be part of a big goal.

_____ **7.** You have to feel that you are going to win.

_____ **8.** You shouldn't let your passion show during the game.

Vocabulary

See Appendix 2 to review the vocabulary terms.

Dean's sister Jackie is at an audition for a commercial. She is hoping to get a break in her acting career. Complete the sentences and conversations with the correct phrasal verbs in the box. Be sure to use the correct tense and form of the verb.

clear up	dream up	figure out	hand in	kick out
turn up	leave out	let down	pass on	pull off

1. Receptionist: Everyone, please _____ your résumés, photos, and contact information at the front desk.

2. Casting director: And please make sure you don't _____ anything _____. If any of the important information is missing, we will not be able to consider you for the part.

3. Tiffany: There's an audition coming up for an interesting part. You'd be great for it.

   Jackie: Really? Thanks for _____ the information. What's the part?

   Tiffany: Well, you'd be playing a sexy spy who destroys a famous politician.

   Jackie: Sounds perfect!

4. Tran: I heard the casting director wanted to _____ you _____ of the auditions last week. What made him so angry?

   Jackie: That's ridiculous! Who _____ that little story?

5. Jackie: If you choose me, I promise I won't _____ you _____. What do you say?

Casting director: I can't say anything for sure. We're considering several actresses for the part.

6. Receptionist: I can't _____ this _____. If you're Jackie *Baker*, then why did you write Jackie *Bishop* on this form?

Jackie: Oh. Let me _____ that _____. You see, Jackie *Baker* is my *stage* name. You know, the name I use for acting only.

7. Casting director: Listen up, everyone! When the stagehand _____ the music, that means "enter." When he turns it down, that means "exit." Everybody ready?

8. Dean: How was the audition?

Jackie: I'm not sure yet, but I think I _____ it _____! I'm sure I'll get the part!

Grammar 1

Present Perfect Continuous with *For* and *Since*

A. Complete the sentences. Use the present perfect continuous form of the verb in parentheses and for *or* since.

1. John (**go**) __has been going__ to bed at midnight _____for_____ the last 2 weeks.

2. Claire's only sister, Jasmine, (**live**) _____ across the country _____ the past 5 years.

3. Ms. Boyd (**avoid**) _____ any kind of animal products _____ she became a vegetarian.

4. Josh (**see**) _____ Kelli _____ 2 months, ever _____ Tuesday, March 5.

5. Amy (**call**) _____ her relatives in Taipei twice a day _____ the earthquake hit Taiwan last week.

B. Circle the correct tense of the verb in each sentence.

1. **Jason:** I **called / have been calling** you at 10:30 last night. Why didn't you answer?

   John: Oh. I **was probably sleeping / 've probably been sleeping**.

2. **Officer Katchem:** Do you realize that **you go / you've been going** 10 miles an hour over the speed limit for the past 2 miles?

   Claire: Sorry, Officer. I'm trying to get to the hospital. My sister **is having / has been having** a baby right now.

3. **Ryan:** **Do you like / Have you been liking** my new leather pants?

   Jenn: Sure. **I've been admiring / I admired** them all day long. They fit so . . . well. And those green stripes are really . . . amazing!

4. **Trisha:** How long **have you been dating / are you dating** Kelli?

   Josh: Oh, **I'm not dating / I haven't been dating** Kelli anymore. We broke up. Thanks for asking, Trish. Maybe we can talk about it sometime.

5. **Tony:** **Were you making / Have you been making** long-distance phone calls from the office phone while I was out of the office last week?

   Craig: I only **made / have been making** one long-distance call—about a month ago.

Grammar 2

Separable Phrasal Verbs

Rewrite the boldfaced part of each sentence. Replace the object with a pronoun (him, her, it, them).

1. **Reporter:** Why did Dean Bishop miss the last match?

   Coach: ~~Dean had to sit out the last game~~ Dean had to sit it out because he had a sore back.

2. **Tony:** Can you **clear up the problem with the tape** before you go home tonight?

   Phil: Sure, Tony. I'll take care of it. Don't worry.

3. **Elisa:** **Would you help out the children** with their homework?

   Tony: Yeah, sure, I will.

4. **Amy:** Are John and Lisa arriving tonight?

   Josh: Yes. Could you please **pick up John and Lisa** at the train station at 8 o'clock.

5. **Coach:** Don't **let your teammates down**: we need you to play in the next game.

   Nick: I promise. I'll be there with you.

Grammar 3

Superlative Adjectives

A. *Every year at the end of the season the players on the national soccer team give awards. Some of the awards are serious and some are funny. Complete the sentences from Coach Haskins's speech at the awards ceremony. Use the superlative form of the adjectives in parentheses.*

1. This year, our award for **(talkative)** ___the most talkative___
    player goes to Colin. He always has something to say!

2. And the award for **(improved)** _____ player
    goes to Hyung. Last year he sat on the bench most of the time.
    But this year he was a key part of our success.

3. Now we all know that one of you guys heads the ball very creatively. The award for **(original)**
    _____ heading style goes to Joe!

4. Let's move to the fashion section. First, the award for **(cool)** _____ haircut
    definitely goes to Brian. Classy shades too, Brian.

5. Now most of you guys get a little stressed when things go wrong, but not you, Johnny! Come
    and accept **(laid-back)** _____ player award.

6. Now the award for the guy who keeps us all laughing, even when things aren't so funny.
    (good) _____ sense of humor award belongs to . . . Ray!

7. Before our final star prize, the man who *thinks* he should win it! Not this year, Dean! But,
    Dean, please come up and accept the award for **(big)** _____ ego.

8. Now, the moment you've all been waiting for. As voted by his own teammates—**(valuable)**
    _____ player award for this year goes to . . . Nick!

B. *Now give awards to your classmates. Use superlatives.*

EXAMPLE: Amal is the most helpful student in the class. She helps everyone with their work.

1. _____

2. _____

3. _____

Language Functions

See Appendix 3 to review the language function charts.

Complete the conversations. Use a specific request for clarification and an idea from the box.

he was part of the plan	we can't get home tonight	I'm not on the team anymore
she doesn't want to go out	you're firing me	you don't want to go anymore

1. **Talia:** I have a feeling that Roshawn knows more than he's saying about this Dean Bishop scandal.

   Amy: _Do you mean that he was part of the plan_____ ?

2. **Claire:** I know it's Saturday, but Talia's got a lot of work to do tonight.

   Josh: _____ ?

3. **Tony:** I don't think we have much more work in the research department.

   Ms. Boyd: _____ ?

4. **Coach:** I'm sure you'll be a better player next season if you keep training.

   Jim: _____ ?

5. **Talia:** I'm afraid my ex-boyfriend is going to be at the party.

   Amy: _____ ?

6. **Josh:** Oh, no! There goes the last train.

   Tom: _____ ?

Application Activities

Study Tip
Review! Look back through the units. Review at least 10 of the exercises and 5 of the Application Activities.

1. **Vocabulary.** Go back through the vocabulary from all the units you have studied. Choose at least 10 words and make a vocabulary test. Don't forget to make an answer key. Exchange tests with a classmate.

2. **Grammar.** Prepare a short survey of 3 different topics, such as ways of spending free time, attitudes about marriage, ways of dealing with stress, and plans for the future. Give your survey to at least 5 people in your class or outside your class. Describe the results of your survey, using as many superlative statements as you can. For example, *(Ji-Eun) is the most (energetic) because she plays soccer 5 days a week.*

3. **Writing.** Think about Coach Haskins's speech in the Task Listening section of the CD-ROM course. What is your "coaching philosophy" on life? What does "success" mean to you? Which successful people do you admire, and why?

4. **Speaking.** Talk to people about important issues in the news or in their personal lives. (Possible topics: health, fashion, politics, sports, relationships, study, work.) When you are listening, be sure to ask clarifying questions.

5. **Project.** You have now completed *Longman English Interactive* (Level 3) and have learned a lot of English. Form a group with 3 or 4 classmates and plan a "motivational seminar." Plan a 5-minute group presentation on ways to learn English better. Each person on your team should present 1 part of your "motivational seminar." If you like, you can also give awards to members of the class.

Grammar Explanations

This section contains the same grammar explanations that are found on the CD-ROM. They are included here for your quick reference. To view the animated presentation, go to the Grammar section of Unit C.4 in the CD-ROM course.

Grammar 1: Present Perfect Continuous with *For* and *Since*

1. We use the **present perfect continuous** to talk about something that **began in the past and is still happening**.
   > **Coach:** The Soccer Federation **has been calling** me for the past 2 days.

   This means that the federation started calling the coach 2 days ago and that they are still calling him.

2. We form the **present perfect continuous** with *have* or *has* + *been* + the **base form** of the verb + *-ing*.
   > I **have been playing**.
   > You **have been playing**.

   Remember, in conversation we often use contractions with pronouns and nouns.
   > **Coach: You've** been having money problems.

   We also use contractions in negative statements with *have not* and *has not*.
   > Nick really **hasn't** been having money problems.

3. We often use the **present perfect continuous** with *for* plus a **length of time**. Some examples of a length of time are *20 minutes, 4 years,* and *a long time*.
   > **Coach:** Nick, we've **been working** together **for 4 years**.

   This means that Nick and the coach started working together 4 years ago and that they are still working together.

4. We also use the **present perfect continuous** with *since* plus the **point of time** when the situation started. Some examples of a point of time are *4:00 p.m., last night, 2001, January*.
   > **Nick:** **I've been trying** to speak to you **since last night**, Coach.

   This means that Nick started trying to speak to his coach last night and that he is still trying.

5. We ask **questions** with *How long* plus the present perfect continuous to find out the **length of time** something has been happening.
   > **Coach: How long have** we **been working** together, Nick?
   > **Nick:** Four years.

Grammar 2: Separable Phrasal Verbs

1. **Phrasal verbs** are verbs that have 2 parts—a **verb** plus a **particle**.
   > *Sit out* is a phrasal verb.

   Sit is the verb; *out* is the particle.

   The particle looks just like a preposition, but it is actually 1 part of this 2-part verb. The particle often changes the meaning of the verb.
   > **Coach:** You mean you didn't take a bribe to **sit out** the game?

   In the example, *sit out* means "not play." As you can see, the verb *sit* plus the particle *out* means something completely different from the verb *sit* by itself.

2. Some phrasal verbs are **separable**. This means that **the noun object can come either after the 2 parts of the verb . . .**
   > **Coach:** Why don't you **clear up this whole thing**?

   . . . or the noun object can come **between the 2 parts** of the verb.
   > **Coach:** Why don't you **clear this whole thing up**?

3. When the object of a phrasal verb is a **pronoun** (a word like *him, her,* or *it*), it **must** go between the verb and the particle.
   > **Talia:** Why didn't you play in the first-round qualifying game?
   > **Nick:** I sat out the game because I had a sprained ankle.
   > I **sat it out** because I had a sprained ankle.

   We do **NOT** say: ~~I sat out it~~.

Grammar 3: Superlative Adjectives

1. We use **superlative adjectives** to compare **3 or more** people or things. When we use superlative adjectives, we are saying that a person or thing has **the most** or **the least** of a certain quality, compared to the other members of the group.
   > **Coach:** You're **the strongest** player on the team, Nick. You're also **the most dependable** of all the players. You really are **the best**!

2. There are several ways to **form the superlative**. For **short adjectives**, we use *the* + **adjective** + *-est*.
   > bright—**the brightest**
   > hard—**the hardest**
   > small—**the smallest**

   Sometimes, when we add *-est*, there are **spelling changes**.
   > nice—**the nicest**
   > big—**the biggest**
   > crazy—**the craziest**

3. A few adjectives have **irregular superlative** forms.

    good—**the best**
    bad—**the worst**

4. For **long adjectives**, we usually form the superlative with ***the most***.

    Dean: You're **the most popular** player on the team.

We can also make a superlative with ***the least*** (the opposite of *the most*).

    Coach: Carl is **the least dependable** player on the team.

5. Some adjectives have 2 possible superlative forms.

    quiet—**the quietest**
    OR **the most** quiet

Appendix 1: Audioscript

Unit A.1

Track 1

Amy: Good morning, Talia. Good MORNing, Talia.
Talia: Oh, hi. Good morning.
Amy: You know, you're working too hard.
Talia: I know. I always work this hard. Maybe you could mention that to Tony? I don't think he knows it.
Amy: Is that a new hairstyle? It's very . . . unique.
Talia: Very funny. I had to work late last night. I'm tired, I'm in a bad mood, and I don't care about my hair.
Amy: That's probably why you're not a reporter yet.
Talia: You think so?
Amy: No, I'm just kidding . . .
Talia: You may be right.
Amy: Maybe Tony will take you more seriously after you finish the journalism class.
Talia: Oh, no! Our journalism class! I forgot. It's tomorrow. What's the homework?
Amy: Compare 2 news stories on the same topic.
Talia: That's easy enough to do. Sounds interesting, too. I guess I'll do it after work.
Amy: You work too hard.

Track 2

Amy: Why don't you take a break tonight? Yeah, why not come with me to a party?
Talia: No, thanks. Maybe some other time.
Amy: Come on! Josh Taylor is having a party. A lot of available guys will be there . . . You might meet someone.
Talia: No, listen! I'm too busy to go. Go without me . . .
Tony: Good, you're here. I have something important to talk to you about. What are you working on?
Talia: I'm researching the background information for that transportation story.
Amy: She's always working. She told me to tell you that.
Tony: I have a big project for you to work on. I know you've been hoping for a break. This may be it.
Talia: Really? That's great!
Tony: Come to my office in about 10 minutes. By the way, you look different. Have you done something with your hair?

Track 3

Good evening, everybody. Is everyone here? OK. Good. Now, tonight we're going to talk about the 1 thing you need to create the best news stories. Do you know what that is? No, I'm not talking about luck! The thing that creates good news stories is curiosity—your own curiosity. Curiosity is the engine, the power for the story. Curiosity will help you come up with good questions.

Now, remember, first you have to start with the 5 classic journalistic questions—you know: *who, what, when, where,* and *why.* Right? We've talked about these a lot. But these questions are just for starters. They're useful questions, but they're not sufficient by themselves. You have to expand on them. You have to get into probing questions. For example, Who else knows that? What do you think about this? When did you first find out about this? Where did you get your information? Why do you care about this? These are the kinds of questions that will shape your story. And you need to develop this kind of curiosity for every story you work on.

Unit A.2

Track 4

Tony: Someone sent us this tape. This is incredible. What a shame.
Talia: What's a shame?
Tony: Have you ever heard of Nick Crawford, the soccer player? He's the star forward on our national team.
Talia: Of course. Everyone's heard of him, I think.
Tony: Well, apparently this conversation took place a while ago: Nick Crawford talks about how he needs money.
Amy: That's not big news. There's a rumor that he's fallen into debt lately. I've heard all sorts of gossip about that.
Tony: Yes, but it gets even more interesting. Also on the tape, a woman offers him $50,000.
Talia: What for?
Tony: To sit out the first-round qualifying match. Remember? Nick Crawford had an injury and he couldn't play in that game?
Talia: Sure, I remember. We lost that match and if we lose again, we might be eliminated.
Tony: Exactly. The next qualifying round is coming up. If this tape is real, Nick Crawford will be history.
Amy: You mean, he won't get to play in the next match?
Tony: Exactly. And without him, we'll probably lose—again.
Amy: Wow! A real scandal! Is the tape for real?
Tony: Talia, that's your job now. Find out if the tape is authentic. And you'd better find out fast.

Track 5

Tony: Is there a problem?
Talia: Not exactly. I'll do it. It's just that . . . I know Nick Crawford.
Tony: You do?
Talia: Yes. We went to college together. It's hard to believe he would do something like this.

Tony: Well, wake up and smell the coffee, Talia! He's a big star. He's been a star on the national team for 4 years now. People do crazy things when they get famous.

Talia: I just can't believe it. Nick Crawford taking a bribe?

Tony: Listen, Talia. You're smart. You're a good researcher, and one day—I hope—you'll be a great reporter. But don't let your emotions get in the way of your work. If you do, I'll have to find someone else to work on this story.

Track 6

In the spotlight on this TV minute is Lance Armstrong, "the Golden Boy of Cycling."

Lance Armstrong was born on September 18, 1971, in a small Texas town. From early on, it was clear that he was a natural athlete. In 1984, at age 13, Lance won a national triathlon, excelling at running, swimming, and bicycling. By 1987, while he was still in high school, Lance had turned professional. He decided to focus exclusively on bicycling, saying, "I was born to race bikes."

Between 1988 and 1996, Armstrong won numerous international races. In January 1996 he was the top-ranked cyclist in the world. Then, during a race in October of that year, Armstrong fell off his bike in excruciating pain. They discovered that he had cancer, which had spread to his lungs and brain. Given only a 50 percent chance of surviving, in 1997 Armstrong underwent difficult cancer treatment. Amazingly, he not only survived, he returned to competition, winning several major races in 1998.

Since that time, Armstrong has gone on to win many more races, including the Tour de France in 1999, 2000, and 2001. Lance says that cancer was an unexpected gift. "I used to ride my bike to make a living. Now I just want to live so that I can ride."

Unit A.3

Track 7

Woman: We'll pay you $50,000.

Nick: And all I have to do is sit on the bench?

Woman: That's right. Do that, and $50,000 is yours.

Nick: Well, I can really use the money. You've got yourself a deal.

Woman: Great. It's a pleasure doing business with you.

Tony: How's it going?

Talia: I can't tell. I hope our expert will be able to figure it out.

Tony: Me, too. When will we have the results?

Talia: He's going to call me back this afternoon.

Tony: Good.

Talia: You know, I've been a researcher here for 3 years. I've investigated other scandals. But something here doesn't seem right.

Tony: What do you mean?

Talia: It just doesn't make sense. Nick Crawford loves soccer. Why would he do something to hurt his career?

Tony: That's a good question. How well do you know Nick Crawford? Is he a friend of yours?

Talia: No, not really. I just knew him in college. We had English together for 2 semesters.

Tony: Oh, that's it?

Talia: Well, I got to know him a little. I know that he moved here from England about 10 years ago. I know that he's smart. And I know that he's always dreamed of being a great soccer star.

Tony: Mm-hmm.

Talia: So, why would he risk ruining his career?

Track 8

Talia: Tony, listen. I have an idea. Let me go and talk to Nick.

Tony: I don't know . . .

Talia: He may remember me. He may be willing to confide in me.

Tony: Talia, look, you're not a reporter yet, you're still a researcher. Remember?

Talia: Please, Tony. Give me a chance. What do you have to lose?

Tony: OK, I'll give you 1 more day. But only 1 more day.

Talia: You won't be sorry. Just 1 more thing: If I find something big, the story is mine, right?

Tony: What do you mean?

Talia: I mean, you'll let me report it, won't you? If I can get Nick to tell me everything?

Tony: You deserve a break. I know that. I'll tell you what: Come up with something big and the story is yours. But, Talia, be careful.

Talia: What do you mean?

Tony: This Nick Crawford guy . . . I hear he can be very charming. Don't let him charm you out of a story.

Track 9

Message 1, 2:27 p.m.
Hello, this is Bill Brown, from the City Transportation Department. I'm returning your call from Friday. I have most of the figures you requested, and I should have the rest of the information by tomorrow. Please call me back before tomorrow afternoon, and give me your fax number. My number is 572-0900, extension 412. Again, this is Bill Brown and the number is 572-0900, extension 412. Thank you.

Message 5, 11:45 a.m.
Hello. This is a message for Tony Grimaldi. This is Larry Pugo, that's P-U-G-O, from Ace Entertainment in New York. I have some information related to a story you're investigating. Please call me back . . . I'll give you my private line. It's 982-7440. Again, it's 982-7440. The best time to reach me is between 4:00 and 6:00 today. Thanks.

Message 2, 1:59 p.m.
Amy, this is Josh . . . Josh Taylor . . . sorry to bother you at work. I wanted to get in touch with you, and I lost your email address . . . and anyway, I just wanted to find out if you and your friend Talia are coming to the party tonight. Give me a call on my cell phone if you get a chance . . . I'm at 437-8834. That's 437-8834. See you.

Track 10

Talia: Nick?

Nick: I know you, don't I?

Talia: Yes. I'm Talia, Talia Santos.

Nick: Yeah, Talia! Of course!

Talia: After all these years, I'm surprised you remember me.

Nick: How could I forget you? We were in an English literature class together, weren't we?

Talia: That's right, the Shakespeare class.

Nick: Right, Dr. Custer's class. She was a tough teacher. She really made us work hard.

Talia: Oh, gosh, don't remind me.

Nick: We studied together for the final, didn't we?

Talia: Yes, that's right. As I recall, you did really well on it.

Nick: That's right! But only because I speak Shakespeare so fluently.

Talia: Very cute.

Nick: So, what are you doing here? Are you a big soccer fan now?

Talia: Not exactly. I'm a researcher now . . . with *Newsline*.

Nick: Oh, I see. Well, news people aren't my favorite people right now. I heard that there's a nasty story coming out about me. Something about me throwing a game?

Talia: That's why I'm here.

Nick: Too bad. Well, maybe we can meet again sometime, under different circumstances.

Track 11

Talia: No, listen. I'd like to . . . I want to hear your side of the story. You don't trust me, do you?

Nick: Nope. You're in the news business. You're all alike.

Talia: Hey, don't judge me so quickly. I told you the truth about why I was here, didn't I? Really. You can trust me.

Nick: Look, the only goal I have right now is helping my team win the qualifying match next weekend. After that, I will deal with this mess.

Talia: Wait, Nick. The charges are serious. People say you threw a game. They think you have gambling debts.

Nick: Yes. That's why I gave the Soccer Federation access to my bank accounts.

Talia: They could stop you from playing. Forever.

Nick: That's impossible.

Talia: No, it's not. That's why I want you to talk to me. I want your story. Did you or didn't you take the money? Did you or didn't you throw the game?

Nick: Oh, you want to hear my story? Do you want to hear the true story or the story that will get your show more viewers? Which story do you really want? Take your pick.

Talia: The only story I want is the true story.

Nick: Well, the truth is, I didn't do it. I'm an innocent man.

Track 12

Come one, come all and tune in this week, every night, from 10 to 11 p.m. for our Great Authors series. Each night this week is dedicated entirely to the master playwright and poet William Shakespeare. On Monday, we set the scene with a look at the life and times of Shakespeare in England, from his birth in 1564 to his death in 1616. On Tuesday, we'll examine the fanciful comedies of Shakespeare, including *A Midsummer Night's Dream* and *All's Well That Ends Well*. On Wednesday, we'll have a look at Shakespeare's historical plays, including *Julius Caesar* and *Richard III*. On Thursday, bring your handkerchiefs and join us as we sample some of Shakespeare's great tragedies, including *Hamlet* and *Romeo and Juliet*. And, finally, on Friday, we'll experience the real Shakespeare in love, with an in-depth exploration of Shakespeare's romantic poetry, including "A Lover's Complaint," and a selection from his 154 sonnets. Remember, this week, beginning Monday, from 10 to 11 p.m.—experience the stuff that great literature is made of. That's Channel 10, your public service cable channel for history, drama, education, and culture.

Unit B.1

Track 13

Talia: OK, let's get this straight. You're one of the country's best soccer players . . .

Nick: Well, I have to admit—that's true. Of course, some people think that's not such a great achievement.

Talia: Now, for some reason, you sat out one of the biggest games of the year.

Nick: Not just for some reason. I sat out because I had a sprained ankle. I could hardly walk. I certainly couldn't play.

Talia: But your coach can't verify this.

Nick: Of course not. You can't see a sprain on an X-ray.

Talia: You can't?

Nick: No.

Talia: I see . . .

Nick: You don't have to believe me, but it's the truth. I sat out the first-round qualifying match because I had a sprained ankle.

Talia: And not because you took a bribe?

Nick: A bribe? How can anybody believe such a ridiculous thing?

Talia: Then can you explain the tape?

Nick: What tape?

Talia: Listen to this.

Woman's voice: We'll pay you $50,000.

Nick's voice: And all I have to do is sit on the bench?

Woman's voice: That's right. Do that and $50,000 is yours.

Nick's voice: Well, I can really use the money. You've got yourself a deal.

Woman's voice: Great. It's a pleasure doing business with you.

Track 14

Nick: It sure sounds like my voice, but I don't know why. Why would I do something so stupid?

Talia: That's what I want to know.

Nick: Hey, Coach! Can I talk to you for a minute? Some TV station is going to report that I deliberately sat out a game!

Coach: I know all about it. Who is this?

Nick: This is an old friend of mine from college, Talia Santos. She works for *Newsline*. This is Coach Haskins, and you may recognize my teammate, Dean Bishop.

Dean: Hey.

Coach: Hi.

Talia: Nice to meet you both.

Coach: Would you excuse us for a moment, please?

Talia: Sure.

Coach: Look, I don't think it's such a good idea to talk to the media right now.

Dean: Yeah, you've got that right.

Nick: Coach, I just don't get it. Why would anybody try to do this to me?

Coach: Well, we're going to find that out. I don't want to worry you, Nick, but I've been getting some pressure from the Soccer Federation.

Nick: What do you mean?

Coach: They want you to sit out the game next week.

Dean: No!

Nick: They can't do that!

Coach: Yes, they can. Nick, I know how badly you want to play, and, frankly, I don't think we can win without you.

Track 15

Thank you for contacting Health Web. Please click on the type of advice you need . . . Thank you, you have selected: Sprained ankles.

Sprained ankles are a very common injury. A sprain occurs when you suddenly stretch or tear one of the three ligaments around the ankle. We suggest the following treatment.

First, carefully remove your shoe and sock.

Next, compress the ankle by wrapping an elastic bandage 2 times around the sprained ankle. The bandage should be snug, but not too tight.

Then apply an ice bag. Place the ice on top of the bandage, not directly on your skin. Ice prevents further swelling.

After that, elevate the ankle so that it is higher than your heart. This will help reduce the pain.

If you are in a lot of pain, take an over-the-counter pain medication.

After 30 minutes, try to stand, but don't put too much weight on the ankle. Move the ankle around slowly. Movement is important so the ankle doesn't become stiff.

Continue to apply an ice bag on the ankle for 20 minutes, every 2 hours, throughout the next day. This will help promote healing. Rest your ankle for 24 to 48 hours.

This treatment is called the RICE treatment, R-I-C-E: R is for rest, *I* is for ice, *C* is for compression, and *E* is for elevation.

Unit B.2

Track 16

Tony: And sometimes people do things just because they can. Take it from me. I've seen a lot of people do stupid things. Even rich, famous people. It may not always make sense.

Talia: But, except for that tape, we have no proof . . .

Tony: We had no proof. We have it now. Amy, tell her.

Amy: I'm sorry, Talia. The audit of Nick's bank account came in. He deposited $50,000 in his bank account a week before the qualifying match.

Talia: Oh, my gosh. What? Let me see that. I'm not going to stop investigating. There might be a good explanation for this.

Track 17

Tony: You can keep investigating, but after looking at this bank statement, we have no choice. We're going with this story tonight. If we don't, the competition may beat us to it.

Amy: You've got to admit, Talia, it doesn't look good.

Talia: I keep telling myself we're missing something. Things aren't always as they seem.

Tony: And sometimes things are exactly the way they seem.

Talia: I just don't think that's true in this case.

Tony: You just may be too trusting to be a reporter. Reporters have to be skeptical. Are you sure you're all right working on this by yourself? Maybe you should work with John Donnelly.

Talia: No. I can do this myself. I promised Nick I'd be fair. I promised you I wouldn't let my emotions color my judgment. And I promised myself I'd do a good job.

Tony: OK. But if you let me down, I'm giving the story to John.

Talia: Thanks, Tony. I'll be fine. You won't be sorry.

Track 18

Host: Welcome to *Star Talk*. Today's topic is privacy. Should entertainers—movie stars, singers—have the right to privacy? Let's take our first call. Hello, caller number 1.

Caller 1: Hello. I'm a big movie buff, and I read all the entertainment magazines. I love reading about movie stars and their private lives. Ordinary people want to know what the stars are up to— that's only natural! But on the other hand, I can understand why some stars get angry when reporters and photographers reveal all their embarrassing secrets. Everyone needs a little privacy . . . even movie stars!

Unit B.3

Track 19

Talia: There you are! Nick, are you going to stop lying to me?

Nick: Hello, Talia. And how are you? Would you like to have a seat?

Talia: No, actually, I prefer to stand.

Nick: OK. Whatever. So now what's going on?

Talia: This! $50,000 appeared in your bank account just before the qualifying match. $50,000!

Nick: So?

Talia: So? So that's exactly the amount of money they say you accepted for throwing that game.

Nick: It's also the exact amount of money I got for endorsing a new line of athletic shoes.

Track 20

Jackie: Excuse me. Aren't you Nick Crawford?

Nick: Yes, that's right. Do I know you?

Jackie: No. Not yet, that is. I'm Jackie Baker. I'm the VP of Marketing for Kicks Shoes.

Nick: Uh-huh.

Jackie: And I have a very interesting proposition for you.

Nick: Keep going. I'm listening.

Jackie: Why don't we meet at my office tomorrow? Let's say, 12:30. We can have lunch nearby, and I'll tell you all about the deal.

Track 21

Sweet-Aid

I love Sweet-Aid
It's pretty and it's pink
I love Sweet-Aid
It's the coolest drink
I love Sweet-Aid
The taste is so "Wow!"
I love Sweet-Aid
I've gotta have some now.

Auntie Nell Donuts

I wanna be an Auntie Nell donut,
I really really really wanna be
If I were an Auntie Nell donut,
All the world would be in love with me.

Laura's Secret

Laura's Secret, just a touch is fine
Laura's Secret, nothing can compare
Laura's Secret, your locks will really shine
Everyone will talk about your hair

Unit B.4

Track 22

Talia: Hello. I'm here to see Jackie Baker.

Receptionist: Hmmm. I don't think . . . I know who you want. Jack Baxter. He's on the third floor, 301 . . .

Talia: No, I'm here to see Jackie Baker, Ms. Jackie Baker.

Receptionist: . . . No, definitely not. There's no one here by that name.

Talia: This is The Gower Building? 119 Gower Street?

Receptionist: Yes. But like I said, there's no Jackie Baker here.

Talia: Well, maybe she's no longer here. Maybe she used to work here.

Receptionist: I don't think so. I've been here for 10 years. Ten years too long, I might add. Someone named Jacob Banker used to work here. Funny, he was an architect, not a banker. Anyway, he was on the second floor . . . Are you sure you're not looking for Jacob Banker?

Talia: No. No. The name is Jackie Baker. She's a VP at Kicks Shoes.

Receptionist: Ahh, now I really don't know what you're talking about. Kicks Shoes? Hold on a second. I'm sorry, but I've never heard of Kicks Shoes and they're not in our directory. Are you sure you're in the right place?

Talia: No. I'm not sure where I am. In fact, I'm not sure about anything anymore.

Track 23

Talia: Oh, no. My cell phone is dead. Can I use your phone for a moment?

Receptionist: You seem really angry. Are you going to yell at someone?

Talia: I don't know. Maybe. Probably . . . Yes.

Receptionist: In that case, be my guest. Just dial 9 first. Uh-oh. Someone's in big trouble.

Nick: Hello.

Talia: Hello, Nick. It's Talia. Remember me?

Nick: Of course I remember you.

Talia: I wasn't sure. You seem to have trouble with names. And faces. And facts.

Nick: Really? I used to have a good memory. I remembered you, didn't I?

Talia: There is no Jackie Baker here. There has never been a Jackie Baker here. And to make matters worse, they've never even heard of Kicks Shoes.

Nick: That's ridiculous! You've got her business card. You're at the Gower Building?

Talia: That's right.

Nick: But I met Jackie there. I met her there. She took me to lunch . . . Have you tried calling her?

Talia: I called before I came, but I got voicemail. One of those messages like, "The person you are calling is not available." I thought it was odd.

Nick: Look, Talia, I don't know what I can say. I'm telling the truth.

Talia: Well, someone is lying. And if you think you're going to see a good story on *Newsline*, you're wrong. Good-bye, Nick.

Receptionist: Oh, that was good.

Track 24

Visitor 1

Receptionist: Hello, can I help you?

Visitor: I'm looking for the office of William Meyer, MDG Records.

Receptionist: Yes, MDG Records is on the fifth floor. William Meyer is in Suite 505.

Visitor: Thanks. 505?

Receptionist: Yes, take the B bank of elevators, get off at the fifth floor, and the office will be on your right.

Visitor: Thank you.

Receptionist: First, could you sign in, please? And can I see some identification?

Visitor 2

Receptionist: Yes, can I help you find someone?

Visitor: I have an appointment with Lucille Cross.

Receptionist: And she would be with . . . ?

Visitor: With Crescent Accounting.

Receptionist: Yes, that's on the twelfth floor. Suite 1201.

Visitor: Twelfth floor?

Receptionist: Yes, take the C bank of elevators to the twelfth floor, and you'll see Crescent Accounting on your left.

Visitor: Thanks.

Receptionist: Just a moment. They like me to call up first . . . your name is . . . ?

Unit C.1

Track 25

Nick: Jackie Baker, please.

Receptionist: Oh, I'm sorry, but there's no Jackie Baker here.

Nick: Do you mind if I look at that?

Receptionist: Not at all. Have a look. . . . Let me guess. You're Nick.

Nick: That's right, but . . . how did you know?

Receptionist: Oh, you're famous!

Nick: Oh. Do you follow soccer?

Receptionist: Soccer? No, never watch it. I was listening when that woman called you. I overheard everything.

Nick: Well, that's great.

Receptionist: She was really angry. Wow!

Nick: I know. I know. Say, do you know what time it is?

Receptionist: Nearly 5. I was just getting ready to leave when you arrived.

Nick: It's probably too late anyway. The news is going to be on in an hour.

Track 26

Receptionist: So, Nick, is there anything else I can do for you?

Nick: Yeah, maybe. Could I speak to someone else at Kicks?

Receptionist: Excuse me?

Nick: Kicks Shoes. May I speak to someone else at Kicks Shoes?

Receptionist: Sorry, Nick, but there's no Kicks Shoes here, either. In fact, I've never even heard of them before today.

Nick: I don't understand.

Receptionist: Cheer up. Things can't be as bad as they seem.

Track 27

And now for this year's casual chic fashions from Eve Landon . . .

First off, here's Michelle, looking perky and cute in her plum-colored shirt and matching plum bag. Speaking of matching, don't you love the way her beige over-the-knee skirt matches her beige shoes? And topping it all off, Michelle is wearing a blue denim jacket with turned-back cuffs . . . very chic . . . thank you, Michelle.

Here's Liz, looking really cool in her black cropped pants. Liz has on a sky-blue cardigan over a gray, scooped-neck, long-sleeved sweater. To complete her outfit, she's carrying an oversized black tote, with plenty of room for her cell phone, water bottle, books, and personal stuff. Fantastic, Liz!

And here's Shanika, with a fresh, sophisticated look. Shanika has on a gray just-above-the-knee slim skirt and black sandals—the perfect shoes for the outfit! She's wearing a simple beige blouse under a short beige leather jacket. Her black shoulder bag is just the right accessory for this young woman on the go. Thanks, Shanika.

Unit C.2

Track 28

Patty: Hey, Nick. It's good to see you again. What can I get for you?

Nick: Could I get a large pineapple and strawberry smoothie?

Patty: Coming right up. Is everything all right?

Nick: My life is a mess! And just when I thought things were going great.

Patty: What's the matter? Did you get hurt?

Nick: Yeah, I got hurt. But not on the soccer field.

Patty: Really?

Nick: Yeah. It all started when I agreed to endorse some shoes. Patty, would you mind making it louder? I need to catch up on the news.

Patty: No problem.

Reporter: . . . Let's see if he's got some comments about this scandal. Hey, Dean! Dean! What do you think about the Nick Crawford scandal?

Dean: I'm not going to comment until we know more.

Reporter: Oh, do you think the Soccer Federation is going to suspend him from playing?

Dean: Well, I really can't say. I'm sure they'll decide as soon as they have more information.

Reporter: What kind of information do you think they'll need to find?

Dean: It's hard to say . . .

Nick:	Hold on. Do you see that woman? The woman standing behind Dean? That's her!
Patty:	That's who?
Nick:	I think that's Jackie Baker! The woman with Kicks Shoes.

Track 29

Patty:	Jackie Baker? No. That's Jackie Bishop, Dean's sister. She was a member here last year, but I haven't seen her around lately. I'm surprised you never ran into her.
Dean:	I've always admired Nick Crawford. I'm sure he wouldn't risk ruining his career.
Nick:	That's her. That's Jackie Baker.
Patty:	No, I'm pretty sure that's Jackie Bishop.
Nick:	But there's something different. No glasses. And her hair . . .
Patty:	Ah. It's blonde now, but she keeps changing the color. She's a wannabe actress.
Nick:	A wannabe actress?
Patty:	Oh yeah! She's tried out for a lot of movie parts, but I doubt she's actually ever acted in anything.
Nick:	Except for the day she took me to lunch. She's a great actress. She should get an Oscar for her performance.

Track 30

Welcome to *Healthy Pleasures,* the TV cooking show that helps you eat right and eat light. Today's show has a tropical theme, so just imagine the palm trees swaying and the orchids blooming all around you.

OK. So first, we're going to prepare a Summer Sling smoothie. For this, we're going to need our blender—which we have right here—by the way, this recipe is for 6 people, so you'll need to cut the ingredients if you're serving 2 or 4. First, we're going to start with the fruit—ripe bananas and luscious papaya. Take 3 peeled bananas and a sliced papaya and put them in the blender. Then we're going to add 2 cups of vanilla yogurt and a cup of crushed ice. Put the lid on the blender, set it to *Blend,* and in just a couple of minutes, you've got a perfectly delicious and nutritious Summer Sling smoothie.

Next, we're going to prepare an Avocado Dream sandwich. Take 2 slices of whole grain bread . . . lay 1 of them on the counter. Now put on 3 very thin slices of Swiss cheese and then 4 slices of avocado, next to each other . . . that's right . . . and now top it with 2 slices of tomato, 4 slices of cucumber . . . and, finally, put on a tablespoon of prepared salsa—it's my secret ingredient! Then put on the top slice of bread and presto! There you have it—an Avocado Dream sandwich. Fantastic! Well, that's all the time we have today, so for . . .

Track 31

Talia:	I'm so glad I went to that class last night. It was really interesting.
Amy:	Well, Talia, you do look a little better today.
Talia:	Well, I don't feel much better.
Amy:	You know what? You missed a great party the other night. Josh's friend, Matt, was there. I really want to introduce you to him. He's . . .
Talia:	I completely believed him. He can be so persuasive. So convincing. I am so disappointed. I feel like such a fool.
Amy:	Look, Talia, you're no fool. Don't be so hard on yourself.
Talia:	But I was convinced that Nick was being honest.

Track 32

Talia:	I'll give you 2 minutes.
Nick:	You won't be sorry. OK, I went to see her. I went to see Jackie Baker.
Talia:	There is no Jackie Baker.
Nick:	That's right.
Talia:	So you admit that you lied?
Nick:	No, I didn't lie. No, listen, this is what happened. . . . She tricked me. She and her brother Dean. They wanted me out of the way. Dean is next in line to be the star player.
Talia:	Wow! This is amazing. So, what are you going to do now?
Nick:	I'm going to the team office to talk to the coach. I've got to make sure he believes me.

Track 33

And now in business news . . . The Houston Orbits of the World Soccer League have just announced that they have signed superstar Elena Gomez to a new contract.

According to a news report from the Orbits, Gomez is now signed through the 2007 season. Her annual salary will be $4.5 million and she will receive a bonus of $1.75 million each year that the Orbits win the league championship.

In addition, Gomez will receive .25 percent of the Orbits ticket sales for home games, and 1% of sales of Orbits sweaters that are emblazoned with her well-known number, 00.

As part of the deal, Gomez agrees to appear in all new Orbits Shoes TV commercials and on any other promotional material for the team. The Orbits spokesperson, Mia Walker, says that the Houston organization is "delighted" that they have signed Gomez. Gomez was not available for comment.

In other business news . . .

Unit C.4

Track 34

Nick: Oh, good, you're here. Coach, I've been trying to speak to you since last night. This whole scandal . . .

Coach: Nick, we've been working together for 4 years now. You're my best player, and frankly, Nick, I feel like we're family.

Nick: Thanks, Coach. Me, too.

Coach: I'm sorry. I didn't know you've been having money problems.

Nick: No, I haven't! I hope you don't believe those lies about me. Trust me coach: I have not let you down.

Track 35

Nick: Dean.

Dean: Nick, buddy. Tough rap you're taking. Is there anything I can do to help?

Nick: Yes, there is something you can do. You can tell Coach what really happened.

Dean: Excuse me?

Nick: You know. You can tell him about this scheme of yours.

Dean: Uh, what are you talking about?

Nick: How you and your so talented sister have been plotting for—how long now?

Dean: I don't know what you're talking about.

Nick: Yeah. The two of you dreamed up that fake endorsement deal. That must have taken a lot of planning. I'm impressed. I didn't know you were that smart.

Dean: You're talking crazy now.

Nick: It was you, Dean. I know it was you. I guess you didn't expect me to figure it out.

Dean: Wow, Nick. You've made up quite a story there. In fact, it's one of the craziest stories I've ever heard.

Nick: I don't know how you pulled it off, how you made that tape. But I know it was you and your sister.

Dean: Yeah? This is so typical of you. Always so sure of yourself. Always the most popular guy on the team. Well, you're not so popular now, Nicky boy.

Nick: I know what you did.

Dean: You think you know. But let's see you prove it.

Track 36

OK, let's get started. Today, I want to share my coaching philosophy with you. There are 4 main principles, which I try to instill in my players from the first day of training camp. These principles are very simple to understand but sometimes very hard to achieve.

The first principle is commitment. I tell my players: You must be committed to excellence, committed to constant improvement, committed to doing your best in all circumstances. So, commitment is the first thing.

The second principle is determination. By this, I mean having a strong sense of purpose. You have to be determined not to let failure discourage you. You have to be willing to get back up each time you fall. That's what determination is.

The third principle is teamwork. I tell my players that there's no "I" in the word *team*. We are not interested in individual achievements. We're working for the combined efforts of each individual; we're contributing to the mutual goals of the team. That's teamwork.

Now the fourth principle is attitude, and not just any attitude, but a winning attitude. A winning attitude is the fire in your belly, the will to win, the passion to do whatever it takes to come out on top. And when I teach my players about this winning attitude, I tell them a very important 3-letter word, and this word is *yet*. You see, losers say, "I can't do it." Winners say, "I can't do it *yet*." I want my players to feel that everything is possible with time. This is what I consider the most important part of a winning attitude.

Appendix 2: Vocabulary Terms

Unit A.1

cheerful *adj.* happy and feeling good
Yoko is always cheerful and has a smile for everyone.

confident *adj.* sure that you can do something well
As soon as you feel confident about using the machine, you can begin.

depressed *adj.* very sad
I got really depressed when I was living abroad because I missed my family so much.

energetic *adj.* very active
Vijay's kids are really energetic. I don't know how they can run around so much!

exhausted *adj.* extremely tired
Valeria was exhausted after the long flight from Johannesburg to London.

in a bad mood *prep. phr.* feeling unhappy or angry
He was in a bad mood after the boss criticized his report.

in a great mood *prep. phr.* feeling very happy or pleased
Lani is in a great mood today—she was accepted by the university.

laid-back *idiom* calm or relaxed, with a tendency not to worry about anything
After my vacation on the island, I feel really laid-back!

nervous *adj.* worried or frightened about something and unable to relax
She's nervous about meeting her boyfriend's parents.

relaxed *adj.* more calm and less worried
A walk in the park after work makes me feel relaxed.

tense *adj.* nervous and anxious
Kostas was really tense before his job interview.

Unit A.2

artificial *adj.* not natural, but made by people
The doctor said I shouldn't use sugar, so I switched to artificial sweeteners.

authentic *adj.* proven to be made by a particular person
The painting was an authentic Raphael.

bogus *adj.* (*informal*) not true or real, although someone tries to make you think it is
The police were checking a bogus insurance claim.

crooked *adj.* (*informal*) not honest
Everyone thought the mayor was crooked, but no one could prove it.

dishonest *adj.* not honest
Don't do business with that company. Their salespeople are dishonest.

fake *adj.* made to look like a real material or object in order to deceive people
She spent a lot of money on an antique and found out later that it was a fake.

for real *idiom* (*spoken*) used to say that someone is or does exactly what they say, even though it is difficult to believe
It's hard to believe, but he's for real—he's done everything he says he has.

phony *adj.* (*informal*) false or not real, and intended to deceive someone
The thief used a phony ID card to gain entry into the office.

sincere *adj.* honest and true, or based on what you really feel or believe
He gave her a sincere apology after missing their appointment.

trustworthy *adj.* able to be trusted or depended on
She'll keep her promise; she's completely trustworthy.

Unit A.3

business *n.* the activity of buying or selling goods or services
A large part of our business is with companies from South America.

businesslike *adj.* effective and practical in the way you do things
Isabelle's attitude was completely professional and businesslike.

competition *n.* the people or groups that are competing against you, especially in business
Our main competition is a company in Shanghai.

competitive *adj.* determined to be more successful than other people or companies
Cory was very competitive in school, and she eventually opened her own business.

emotion *n.* a strong human feeling, such as love or hate
His voice was full of emotion when he spoke at his farewell party.

emotional *adj.* making people have strong feelings
The end of the movie was very emotional. Everyone in the theater was crying.

injured *adj.* physically hurt from an accident or attack
Ms. Mbeki's injured ankle was treated by the doctor.

injury *n.* physical harm or damage that is caused by an accident or attack
The injury Hassan received in the accident wasn't very serious.

innocence *n.* the fact of not being guilty of a crime
Police records proved the innocence of the woman.

innocent *adj.* not guilty of a crime
Nobody believed him when he said he was innocent.

nation *n.* a country and its people
The prime minister spoke to the nation on television.

national *adj.* relating to a whole nation rather than to part of it or to other nations
We were proud to see the national team in the parade at the Olympics.

pleasant *adj.* enjoyable, nice, or good
Her pleasant laugh made it fun to be with her.

pleasure *n.* a feeling of happiness, satisfaction, or enjoyment
What kind of books do you read for pleasure?

scandal *n.* something that has happened that people think is immoral or shocking
The politician was involved in a scandal because he accepted expensive gifts from a company.

scandalous *adj.* completely immoral and shocking
TV reporters love to talk about the latest scandalous news from Hollywood.

shame *n.* the feeling of being guilty or embarrassed that you have after doing something that is wrong
Even though he stole from the company, he never felt any shame.

shameful *adj.* so bad that someone should be ashamed
Everyone was deeply embarrassed by her shameful behavior.

truth *n.* the true facts about something
The judge believed that the witness was telling the truth.

truthful *adj.* giving the true facts about something
She swore that what she had said was completely truthful.

Unit A.4

take a hike *idiom* (*spoken*) an impolite expression, said when you want someone to leave
Look, I said you weren't invited, so take a hike!

take a look *collocation* to read something quickly or consider it, especially in order to decide what to do
Here's their proposal. Take a look at it tonight, and we'll discuss it in the morning.

take care *collocation* (*spoken*) to think about what you are doing so that something bad doesn't happen
The roads are very icy, so take care driving.

take it easy *idiom* (*spoken*) used to tell someone to stop being angry or worried and calm down
Take it easy! It wasn't your fault.

take it from me *idiom* (*spoken*) used to emphasize that someone can believe what you are saying because you know the subject you are talking about
Italy is a beautiful country. Take it from me—I lived in Rome for 7 years.

take it or leave it *idiom* (*spoken*) used to say that someone can accept an offer or refuse it, but that there can be no discussion about it
$2,000 is the most I'm willing to pay—take it or leave it.

take place *collocation* to occur, especially after being planned or arranged
The next match will take place in Monte Carlo.

take sides *collocation* to choose to support a particular person or opinion
My brothers argue with each other a lot, but I try not to take sides.

take your pick *idiom* (*spoken*) to select one of several things
There's chocolate, vanilla, and strawberry—take your pick.

take your time *collocation* to do something slowly or carefully without rushing
You can take your time packing—the flight doesn't leave until this evening.

Unit B.1

get ahead *phr. v.* to succeed, especially in your job
She doesn't have many business skills yet, but I'm sure she'll get ahead.

get along *phr. v.* to have a friendly relationship with someone or a group of people
Avi gets along well with all the other students.

get carried away *idiom* to feel things so strongly that you are no longer in control of what you do or say
Dinner was so good that I got carried away and gave the waiter a 30% tip.

get going *collocation* to make yourself do something or move somewhere more quickly
We'd better get going, or we'll be late.

get it *collocation* (*informal*) to make sense of something
Shuichi just didn't get it when Lola told the joke.

get it together *idiom* to be in control of a situation and do things in an organized and confident way
Of course it's a difficult situation, but you'll just have to get it together and do your best.

get out of *phr. v.* to avoid doing something that you have promised to do or are supposed to do
I've got an appointment at 10:00, but I'll see if I can get out of it.

get over *phr. v.* to become healthy again after being sick, or to become happier after an upsetting experience
It took a long time for Nikki to get over losing her job.

get real *idiom* (*spoken*) used to tell someone not to be stupid, when you think that what he or she is saying or doing is not sensible or practical
Get real, Julio, you can't run a marathon—you've never run more than 5 miles!

get through *phr. v.* to manage to deal with an unpleasant situation until it is over
I don't know how I got through that loud party—it was the most unpleasant evening of my life!

Unit B.2

feel for (someone) *phr. v.* to care strongly if someone feels bad
Sharzade felt for the lost, frightened little boy, and she stayed with him until his parents were found.

feel free *collocation* (*spoken*) used in order to say that you are happy if someone wants to do something
Please feel free to borrow my dictionary any time.

feel funny *collocation* feel slightly ill
I've been feeling funny ever since I ate that fish.

feel like (doing something) *collocation* (*spoken*) to want to do something
Hannes doesn't have any plans this weekend, so if you feel like doing anything, give him a call.

feel like (something) *collocation* (*spoken*) to want to have something
I don't care what we have, but Young-Dae says he feels like Indian food.

feel (someone) out *phr. v.* (*informal*) to find out what someone thinks or feels by asking indirectly
You should feel Dad out about using the car this weekend. He wasn't too happy when it got all dirty the last time you used it.

feel up to (something) *phr. v.* (*informal*) to feel you can do a particular job or activity
I just don't feel up to going dancing tonight. I think I'll stay home and watch TV.

feel (your)self *idiom* to feel healthy or happy in the way that you normally do
It took a long time to get over the flu, but I'm finally feeling myself again.

Unit B.3

analysis *n.* the careful examination of something in order to understand it better
An analysis of her test results showed that she was perfectly healthy.

analyze *v.* to examine or think about something carefully in order to understand it
Scientists are trying to analyze what went wrong.

announce *v.* to officially and publicly tell people about something
The police announced that the suspect had been arrested.

announcement *n.* an official public statement
The whole country was waiting for an announcement about the results of the election.

appoint *v.* to choose someone for a job, position, etc.
The assistant principal appointed Yussuf to lead the committee.

appointment *n.* the act of choosing someone for a job, position, etc.
The president has been giving a lot of thought to the appointment of a new department head.

combination *n.* two or more different things that are used or put together
A combination of factors led to the choice of Germany as the site of the Soccer World Cup championship.

combine *v.* to put two or more things, ideas, or qualities together
The 3 airlines combined to make 1 giant company.

criticism *n.* the act of judging whether someone or something is good or bad
Teresa's criticism of the plan made us reconsider it.

criticize *v.* to judge someone or something severely
The news media criticized the mayor's plan for higher taxes.

develop *v.* to grow or change into something bigger, stronger, or more advanced
We have plans to develop the local economy.

development *n.* the process of becoming bigger, stronger, or more advanced
There's been a lot of economic development in this region recently—just last week, 3 new factories opened up.

endorse *v.* to officially say that you approve of someone or something
After several famous runners endorsed the new shoe, sales rose sharply.

endorsement *n.* officially saying that you approve of someone or something
The president's endorsement is sure to help the senator get reelected.

press *v.* to push against something
Just press the doorbell, and I'll come down and let you in.

pressure *n.* an attempt to make someone do something by using influence, threats, etc.
The group is putting a lot of pressure on the governor to change her mind.

proposal *n.* a plan or idea that is officially suggested for someone to consider
The city government has made a proposal to build several new schools.

propose *v.* to officially suggest that something be done
The group proposed to hold its next meeting in April.

react *v.* to behave in a particular way because of what someone has done or said to you
Ivor didn't react well to the news of his former girlfriend's marriage.

reaction *n.* something that you feel or do because of what has happened to you or been said to you
What was her reaction when you told her?

recommend *v.* to advise someone to do something
I recommend that you try the chicken Kiev—it's very good here.

recommendation *n.* advice given to someone, especially about what to do
Mona's recommendation is that we go hiking tomorrow, because it might rain today.

Unit B.4

holler *v.* (*informal*) to shout loudly
Mom hollered at me to come down to dinner.

mumble *v.* to say something too quietly or not clearly enough for someone to understand you
She mumbled her address, so I had to ask her to say it again.

murmur *v.* to say something in a soft quiet voice
He softly murmured her name.

mutter *v.* to speak in a quiet voice, especially when you are complaining about something but do not want other people to hear you
Nina left the office muttering about how much she hated her job.

scream *v.* to make a loud, high noise with your voice, or shout something loudly because you are hurt, frightened, excited, etc.
When the truck almost hit us, Monika screamed, "Look out!"

shout *v.* to say something very loudly
The announcer shouted, "Goal, goal, goal!" when the team scored.

whisper *v.* to speak or say something very quietly, using your breath rather than your voice
It's against the rules even to whisper in the library.

yell *v.* to shout or say something very loudly because you are angry, excited, or frightened
I know you're angry, but please don't yell at me!

Unit C.1

cheer up *phr. v.* to become happier
Cheer up! Tomorrow's a holiday, and we don't have to work!

go for it *idiom* (*spoken*) said when you think someone should do or try something
If you think it's what you want, go for it!

hang in there *idiom* (*informal*) to remain determined to succeed although things are not easy
Hang in there, Jun. The job is sure to get better!

have a heart *idiom* (*spoken*) said when you want someone to be nicer or more helpful
Have a heart, Mom—don't make me go to school on such a hot day!

keep cool *collocation* to remain calm, and not nervous, upset, or excited
It's hard to keep cool when angry customers are shouting at you.

lighten up *phr. v.* (*spoken*) used in order to tell someone not to be so concerned about something
Hey, lighten up . . . it's only a game!

play it by ear *idiom* (*informal*) to decide what to do as things happen, instead of planning anything
Let's just play it by ear about the weekend—we don't have to decide what to do now.

stick to your guns *idiom* to continue to say or do something although people disagree with you
I know some people don't like your proposal, but I think you should stick to your guns.

wait and see *idiom* (*spoken*) used to say that someone should not be anxious because they will find out about something later
We don't know what he'll do, so we'll just have to wait and see.

watch out *phr. v.* to pay attention to what you are doing and not do anything dangerous
Watch out! That knife is very sharp.

Unit C.2

break down *phr. v.* to stop operating
My car broke down again last week; I guess I'd better get a new one.

catch up on *phr. v.* to do something that needs to be done that you have not had time to do in the past
Zhongmei has been gone for a week and has a lot of work to catch up on.

come up with *phr. v.* to think of a plan, reply, etc.
We'll just have to use the old system until we come up with something new.

fall for *phr. v.* to unexpectedly feel romantic about someone
When he visited the family, he fell for his roommate's sister, and they were married soon after.

go ahead *phr. v.* to do something that you have been preparing to do
The boss says it's OK, so go ahead and take the day off.

hold on *phr. v.* (*spoken*) said when you want someone to pause or stop talking, for example, during a telephone call
Hold on for a minute, and I'll check my address book.

look into *phr. v.* to try to find out the truth about something
Police are looking into the fire at the warehouse.

look up to *phr. v.* to have a very high opinion of someone
She always looked up to her older sister.

run into *phr. v.* (*informal*) to meet someone unexpectedly
When we were in the south of France, we ran into Lucille.

try out *phr. v.* to attempt to join a team, get a role as an actor, etc.
The hockey team still needs a few more players. Why don't you try out?

Unit C.3

out of control *collocation* impossible to guide or direct
The car went out of control and ran into a fence.

out of date *collocation* no longer useful or modern
Your map is out of date; it still shows some countries that no longer exist.

out of it *collocation* (*informal*) no longer able to think clearly
I'm really out of it—my flight took 26 hours!

out of place *collocation* not in the correct or usual position
I knew somebody had used my cup because it was out of place on my desk.

out of sorts *collocation* feeling a little angry or unwell
Please don't blame Masako for what she said—she's just feeling out of sorts.

out of the blue *idiom* when you are not expecting something to happen
Someone sent me flowers out of the blue this morning. I was so surprised!

out of the question *collocation* used in order to emphasize that what someone wants to do is not permitted
I know you'd like a few days off, but it's out of the question—we have to meet that deadline!

out of the way *collocation* in a position that is not preventing anyone from moving, succeeding, etc.
He must be glad Nicola resigned. Now that she's out of the way, I'm sure he'll be promoted soon.

out of this world *idiom* used to emphasize that something is very good, large, impressive, etc.
You should try Maribel's cake—it's out of this world!

out of work *collocation* unemployed
Josef has been out of work since his company shut down.

Unit C.4

clear up *phr. v.* to make something easier to understand
We don't know how this happened, but we'd better clear it up so it won't happen again.

dream up *phr. v.* to think of something new and unusual
Who dreamed up the title of that program?

figure out *phr. v.* to manage to make sense of someone or something
Please explain to me why my computer broke down; I just can't figure it out.

hand in *phr. v.* to give something to someone in a position of authority
Please hand your request in to the personnel section by May 15.

kick out *phr. v.* (*informal*) to force someone out of a place
The manager kicked Young-Ran out of the restaurant because she was smoking in the non-smoking section.

leave out *phr. v.* to not include someone or something.
If you leave Achmet out of the party, he'll be awfully disappointed.

let down *phr. v.* to make someone feel disappointed because you have not done what you have promised
You said you'd come to the party. You won't let me down, will you?

pass on *phr. v.* to give someone a piece of information that someone else has told you
Please pass the news on to Arturo when you see him.

pull off *phr. v.* (*informal*) to be successful with something that is not easy
Did you hear that Marcus just graduated from medical school? I'm surprised—I really didn't think he could pull it off.

turn up *phr. v.* to make a machine such as a radio, oven, etc. produce more sound, heat, etc.
Would you mind turning up the air conditioner? It's awfully hot in here.

Appendix 3: Language Functions

Unit A.1

Inviting	
Let's	go out to dinner tonight.
How about	going out to dinner tonight?
Why don't we	
Do you want to	
Want to	go out to dinner tonight?
Would you like to	

Accepting an Invitation	
OK.	Fine.
Sure.	That sounds great.
Great.	That'd be great.
Yes.	That would be very nice.
Thank you.	I'd like that.

Declining an Invitation	
Sorry. I can't.	Maybe some other time.
I'd love to, but	I'm busy. How about Friday?
Unfortunately,	I have other plans.
Thank you, but	I'm not free.

Unit A.2

Telling People News or Gossip	
There's a rumor that	
Apparently,	
Guess what?	
I hear	Nick Crawford has fallen into debt lately.
They say	
Have you heard?	
Listen to this!	

Responding to News or Gossip	
Wow!	You're kidding!
No way!	I don't believe it!
Are you serious?	That's incredible!

Unit A.3

Proposing Your Idea

Listen, Say,	I have an idea.
	can I run something by you?
	I've been thinking about something.

Responding to a Proposal: Hesitating

I don't know . . .	I guess so, but . . .
Hmmm . . .	I suppose so, but . . .
Well . . .	I'm not sure . . .

Convincing

Give me a chance!	It's worth a try.
Oh, come on!	Let me have a shot at it.
What do you have to lose?	

Unit A.4

Confirming That You Know Someone

You don't know the person's name	
Excuse me, but	haven't we met before?
	I think we've met before.
	don't I know you from somewhere?

You know the person's name
Excuse me, but aren't you Marc Adams?
Is your name Marc?
Marc? Marc Adams?

Responding

The person has made a mistake	
No, I'm sorry.	You must be mistaken.
	You must have me confused with someone else.

The person recognizes you, but you don't recognize the person	
Yes, I'm Marc.	I'm sorry. . . have we met before?
Yes, that's right.	And you are . . . ?

Responding

You recognize the person but can't remember the name	
Yes . . .	I think we met at Bruno's party. I'm sorry, but I can't remember your name.
	I'm sorry. You look familiar, but I can't place you.

You recognize the person	
Hi! Frank!	How are you?
	How have you been?
	It's great to see you again!
	Fancy meeting you here!

Giving Orders
Find out if this tape is authentic.
I need you to send this fax for me.
Get Sandy's phone number for me, please.

Making Requests
Could you call Tony today?
Would you mind buying me a cup of coffee at the deli?
Can I ask you to come to my office?
When you get a chance, could you make some copies for me?

Responding: Agreeing	
Order/Request	Agreeing
Please call Tony today.	Sure. OK, no problem. Of course. I'd be glad to.
Would you mind calling Tony today?	No, not at all. No, of course not.

Responding: Refusing or Delaying		
Order	Delay	
Find out if the tape is authentic.	Sorry, but Oh . . . Well, actually, I'd like to, but	I have to take care of this first. Then I can do it. I can't right now. Can I put it off until later?
Request	Refuse	
Could you get Sandy's phone number for me?	Sorry, but Oh . . . Well, actually, I'd like to, but	I'm afraid I can't. I can't. I have to leave now. I'm really busy right now. I'm tied up at the moment.

Unit B.2

Talking about Possibilities	
It's possible that There's a chance that It's likely that	he's in his office now.
Talia might	go to class tonight.

Talking about Possibilities	
Asking about Possibilities	**Responding**
Do you think that Talia will come to the party? Is it possible that Nick took the money? Is there a chance that Tony lost the tape?	Sure. It's possible. Possibly. Maybe. Perhaps. Could be. I don't think so. Not a chance.

Unit B.3

News	Giving Feedback
I just got the new schedule.	Oh? Oh, really? Ah. Uh-huh. Mmm. I see. So?
I'm going on vacation next week.	Good for you! That sounds like fun. That's wonderful. Great!
My grandfather died last week.	How awful. Oh, no! Sorry to hear that. I'm really sorry.

News	Asking Follow-up Questions
I was at a business conference in Washington.	How was it? How did it go? Did you have a good time? What was it like?

Unit B.4

Expressing Certainty	
I know	
I'm positive	Nick did it.
I'm sure	Nick didn't do it.
It's clear to me that	

Expressing Uncertainty	
I'm not so sure that	
I doubt that	Nick did it.
I have trouble believing that	

Confirming	Responding
	I'm sure.
	I'm positive.
Are you sure about that?	Oh, yes. Absolutely.
Are you certain about that?	No doubt about it.
Do you really think so?	I'm pretty sure.
	No, I'm not sure.
	Actually, I really doubt it.

Unit C.1

Asking Permission	
Do you mind if I	
Is it OK if I	
Can I	use your phone?
Could I	
May I	

Offering Help		Accepting
Can I help you		Yes, thanks.
Do you need some help	with that?	Sure. I'd
Do you need a hand		appreciate it.
Let me help you		That's nice of
Maybe I can help you	with that.	you.

Asking Permission	Giving Permission
	No problem.
	Sure, go ahead.
	Fine with me.
	Be my guest.
Is it OK if I use your phone?	Help yourself. [for use of personal items]
	Denying Permission
	Um, I'd rather you didn't.
	Sorry, but (I'm using it right now).
	Giving Permission
Do you mind if I use your phone?	No, I don't.
	Denying Permission
	Well, actually, yes, I do.

Offering Help		Declining
Can I help you		It's all right.
Do you need some help	with that?	No, thanks.
Do you need a hand		That's OK, I can do it myself.
Let me help you		No, but thanks
Maybe I can help you	with that.	anyway.

Unit C.2

Asking for Opinions	
Do you think Do you feel Do you believe	Nick did it?
What do you think of What's your opinion about What are your thoughts on What are your feelings about What do you make of	the Nick Crawford story?

Giving Opinions	
Softening	
Actually, To tell the truth, Frankly,	I (think/believe/feel) he didn't do it.
If you ask me, In my opinion, I'm pretty sure that	he didn't do it.
Avoiding	
You know,	I really can't say. I'm not really sure.
I'd rather not say. I don't have anything to say about that. No comment. [for news conferences]	

Unit C.3

Expressing a Need for Something	
I (really) need I've (really) got to have I (really) have to have	a new computer.
Expressing a Need to Take an Action	
I (really) need to I (really) have to I've (really) got to It's (really) important that I It's essential for me to	finish this assignment.

Asking Questions about a Need for Things
What do you need? (*used when you think someone needs something*)
Do you need something? (*used when you think someone needs something*)
Do you need anything? (*used when you want to be considerate/polite*)
Is there anything you need? (*used when you want to be considerate/polite*)

Asking Questions about a Need for Actions
What do you need me to do? (*used when you think someone needs something*)
Do you need me to do something? (*used when you think someone needs something*)
Do you need me to do anything? (*used when you want to be considerate/polite*)
Is there anything you need me to do? (*used when you want to be considerate/polite*)

(*See next page for another Unit C.3 chart.*)

Questions about General Needs	Responses (Specifying What You Need)
Is there anything you need?	Yes. I need a new computer.

Questions about Specific Needs	Responses (Positive/Negative)
Do you need a new computer?	Yes. Sure. No, thanks. No, that's OK.

Unit C.4

Requesting Clarification about Something Specific	
Do you mean that Are you saying that You're saying that In other words, You mean,	he took the money?

Requesting General Clarification	
Could you clarify that for me?	Could you go over that again?
What do you mean by that?	I'm not quite sure what you're getting at.
What does that mean?	I don't get it.
Can you run that by me again?	

Specific Clarification Request	Responding to the Request	
	Positive	
	Yes, that's what I mean. Exactly. Right.	
Are you saying that he took the money?	**Negative**	**Giving additional information**
	Not really. No, that's not what I mean. Not at all.	What I'm trying to say is, he . . . What I'm getting at is, he . . . Let me put it this way: He . . .

General Clarification Request	Giving Additional Information
Could you go over that again?	Sure. He took the money because . . . What I'm trying to say is, he took the money because . . . What I'm getting at is, he took the money because . . . Let me put it this way: He took the money because . . .

Answer Key

Unit A.1

Listening

A. 2. could
3. had
4. don't care about
5. may
6. What's
7. That's
8. I'll

B. 2. busy
3. working
4. to tell you that
5. big project
6. a break
7. look

C. **Classic questions**
- <u>Who</u> did it?
- <u>What</u> happened?
- <u>When</u> did it happen?
- <u>Where</u> was it?
- <u>Why</u> did it happen?

Probing questions
- <u>Who else</u> knows this?
- <u>What do you think</u> about this?
- <u>When</u> did <u>you first find out</u> about this?
- <u>Where did you get</u> your information?
- <u>Why do you care</u> about this?

Vocabulary

2. He's too depressed for Talia. He's not confident enough for Talia
3. He's too energetic for Talia. He's not laid-back/relaxed enough for Talia.
4. He's too laid-back for Talia. He's not energetic enough for Talia.
5. She's too nervous for him. She's not relaxed enough for him.

Grammar 1

1. 'm talking; wants; 'm working; understand; tell
2. do you know; want; 'm not looking; know
3. are you two laughing, 's working; doesn't have; don't usually have; never do

Grammar 2

A. 2. How about calling our report
3. Let's take a coffee break
4. Why don't we invite him
5. OK
6. why don't you leave work

B. Sample answers:
1. How about having class outside today?
2. Why don't you come to the movies with me tonight?
3. Let's go to the beach this weekend.

Grammar 3

A. 2. Amy writes well enough to pass her journalism class.
3. Amy is nice enough to help Talia.
4. Tony is too busy to talk with Talia now.
5. John Connelly listens carefully enough to do great interviews.
6. There isn't enough time for Talia to take a break.

B. Sample answers:
1. I have enough time to see my friends.
2. I have too much work to leave early.
3. I don't have enough money to buy a house.

Language Functions

A. Sample answers:
2. 'd like to
3. have to work
4. some other time
5. How about
6. free
7. 'm not free then.
8. helping
9. finish
10. let's
11. 'm having
12. Sure.
13. sounds

B. Sample answers:
1. Would you like to go to a concert; have other plans
2. Sorry, I can't. I have to work late tonight.
3. Would you like to have; I'd love to.
4. How about a movie tonight?; Sure. That sounds great.

Unit A.2

Listening

A. 2. Apparently this conversation took place a while ago.
3. There's a rumor that he's fallen into debt lately.
4. I've heard all sorts of gossip about that.
5. Also on the tape, a woman offers him $50,000.
6. If this tape is real, Nick Crawford will be history.
7. You mean, he won't get to play in the next match?

B. 1. problem
2. exactly
3. hard
4. wake up
5. coffee
6. crazy
7. famous
8. smart
9. good
10. great
11. let
12. emotions

C. There are many interpretations of Lance Armstrong's statement. One interpretation is: Now I appreciate the simple things in life, such as riding a bicycle.

Vocabulary

1. fake
2. bogus; crooked; trustworthy
3. authentic
4. actual; real; dishonest
5. authentic; valuable
6. for real; fake
7. artificial
8. phony

Grammar 1

1. have you worked; I've been
2. has *Newsline* been in business; we've built
3. 've recently started
4. Have you ever done; I've reported
5. have you learned; I've had; Lately I've learned

Grammar 2

A. 2. You ought to ask Claire to help you with the story.
   3. Don't let your feelings get in the way of your work.
   4. We'd better/You'd better make a copy of this tape in case something happens to it.
   5. We ought to find out if the tape is authentic.

B. Sample answers:
   2. You'd better go talk to the audio expert right away.
   3. You ought to take a break and eat something.
   4. You shouldn't wait until the last minute next time.
   5. You should go to the party with Amy.

Grammar 3

A. 2. a   5. c
   3. f   6. e
   4. b

B. Sample answers:
   1. This weekend I'm going to go to a movie with some friends.
   2. Next year I will go to business school.
   3. In 5 years I will probably get married.

Language Functions

A. 1. there's a rumor that / they say; OK; That's incredible!
   2. have you heard?; You're not serious! / You're kidding!; OK
   3. Guess what!; I heard; No way!; I don't believe it!
   4. Listen to this!; They say; OK; No way!

B. Sample dialogue:
   Have you heard? Angelina Jolie is coming to our party on Friday!
   No way! That's incredible!

Unit A.3

Listening

A. 3. Tony and Talia
   4. the audio expert
   5. Talia
   6. Nick's
   7. Talia's
   8. Talia and Nick

B. 2. day
   3. sorry
   4. break
   5. what; big; yours
   6. story

C. 1. Bill Brown; the City Transportation Department; the figures; call back; afternoon; 572-0900; 412
   2. Larry Pugo; Ace Entertainment; New York; information; private line; 4:00; 6:00
   3. Josh Taylor; your email address; you and Talia are coming to the party tonight; 437-8834

Vocabulary

3. surprised
4. national
5. pleasant
6. competitive
7. competitions
8. professional
9. business
10. injury
11. shame
12. injured
13. confident

Grammar 1

2. (the current year)
3. have been married
4. (number of years between 1985 and the current year)
5. received
6. 1987
7. went
8. have always tried
9. since
10. did not start
11. started
12. 2
13. got
14. 1995
15. hired
16. has ever had
17. has learned
18. 2000
19. became
20. took

Grammar 2

3. By the time he was a teenager, he could create/he was able to create fashionable dresses and suits.
4. Once when he was 16, he broke his clothing-making record: He was able to finish 10 outfits in 1 day!
5. So many people started coming to his workshop that Qi-Ping couldn't handle/wasn't able to handle all the orders by himself.
6. Qi-Ping was able to borrow money from a bank and opened a small factory. That was his big break.
7. Today, Qi-Ping and the employees of his company, Key Originals, can produce/are able to produce over 500 garments a day.

Grammar 3

2. him	9. our
3. Dean *or* him	10. he
4. him	11. his
5. his	12. His
6. theirs	13. your
7. his	14. me
8. his	

Language Functions

Sample answers:
1. run something; It's worth a try; not sure; come on; Give me a chance; Hmm
2. I've been thinking; I don't know; Oh, come on!

BONUS
Sample dialogue:

You: Listen, I have an idea. Why don't you let me give the presentation at the sales meeting?

Your boss: Hmmm, I'm not sure. You haven't had much experience.

You: Let me have a shot at it. I'll prepare really well!

Your boss: Well, OK. But I'll have to help you with it.

Unit A.4

Listening

A.	2. a	4. c	6. e
	3. g	5. b	7. d

B.	2. the	6. a; ∅
	3. the	7. the
	4. the	8. the
	5. this	9. the

C.
2. Each night this week is dedicated entirely to
3. the master playwright and poet
4. look at the life and times of Shakespeare
5. we'll examine the fanciful comedies
6. Shakespeare's historical plays
7. join us as we sample some of
8. with an in-depth exploration of
9. a selection from his 154 sonnets
10. your public service cable channel

Vocabulary

1. Take a look; take place; Take it; me; take; seat
2. Take; pick; take sides
3. Take it; me; Take; time
4. Take care; Take care

Grammar 1

2. can't you; are you
3. were you
4. isn't she; won't you
5. didn't she
6. could you; don't you

Grammar 2

2. boring
3. late; important
4. directly
5. hard; carefully
6. quietly; angrily
7. early; correctly
8. good/patient; patiently

Grammar 3

2. the	7. ∅	12. a
3. The	8. ∅	13. the
4. the	9. the	14. the
5. the	10. the	
6. ∅	11. the	

Language Functions

A.	2. e	4. c	6. g
	3. a	5. d	7. b

B.	1. but aren't you	4. met before
	2. that's right	5. met
	3. Janet	6. see you again

Unit B.1

Listening

A. (words in correct order)
2. such a
3. could hardly
4. sprained ankle
5. can anybody
6. can you

B. **2.** is going to report   **5.** try to do this
     3. works for   **6.** want you to sit out
     4. such a good

C. **2.** g   **4.** e   **6.** a
     3. b   **5.** c   **7.** f

Vocabulary

     2. gets along   **7.** get over
     3. Get real   **8.** gotten ahead
     4. get out of   **9.** get it together
     5. get carried away   **10.** get going
     6. get through

Grammar 1

Monday: understands; want; Does he really mean
Tuesday: don't have
Wednesday: don't think; think; don't trust; thinks; like;
    don't want
Thursday: looks; has; feel; need
Friday: tasted; put; 'm having

Grammar 2

A. **2.** Would you mind
     3. Can I ask you
     4. return
     5. Would
     6. Will you get me

B. 6   1   5   4   2   3

BONUS
Sample answers:
     1. My friend; Can you help me study for the test?
     2. My boss; Could I have another day to finish the
       project?

Grammar 3

A. **3.** Harold and Mary Crawford were such good
       influences on Nick.
     4. That's why Nick was such an honest child.
     5. Nick was so sweet on our first date.
     6. He brought me such beautiful flowers.
     7. Nick wanted to be on the national team so much.
     8. Sometimes I got so mad at him for being such a
       competitive player.
     9. Nick got so busy when he became a professional.

B. Sample answers:
     1. Kumiko was so shy when she was young. (My
       mother)
     2. Paulo was such a good football player in high
       school. (My high school football coach)

Language Functions

A. **1.** need   **3.** please
     2. chance   **4.** mind

B. Sample answers:
     1. Would you mind giving me Nick's medical report;
       OK, no problem.
     2. I need you to find out if Talia knows Nick well.;
       Sorry, but I'm afraid I can't.
     3. Tell me the truth, Nick!; I'd be glad to.
     4. Could you find out if the report is ready, please?;
       Oh, I have to take care of this first. Then I can
       do it.

Unit B.2

Listening

A. **1.** proof   **5.** deposited
     2. had   **6.** week before
     3. have   **7.** stop investigating
     4. came   **8.** explanation

B. **2.** We're going with this story tonight.
     3. I keep telling myself we're missing something.
     4. You just may be too trusting to be a reporter.
     5. Are you sure you're all right working on this by
       yourself?
     6. I promised myself I'd do a good job.

C. *Caller 1:* buff; entertainment; what the stars are up to;
               natural; reveal; Everyone

Vocabulary

     2. feel for   **5.** feeling; out
     3. feel like   **6.** feel free
     4. feeling myself   **7.** feel funny

Grammar 1

A. don't recall feeling
     looking forward to going
     Taking a bribe
     risk getting caught
     start admitting

B. Sample answers:
     1. I enjoy playing tennis.
     2. I miss going to my favorite restaurant at home.
     3. I keep staying up late to finish studying!

Grammar 2

A. **2.** may/might/could have a cold
     3. may/might/could have another appointment
     4. may/might/could belong to Talia

B. **1.** may/might/could
     2. may/might/could
     3. It may/might/could be

Grammar 3

A. 2. himself   5. yourself
    3. yourselves   6. itself
    4. myself

B. Sample answers:
    1. I talk to myself when I'm alone.
    2. I sing to myself in the shower.
    3. I buy myself clothes when I've had a hard week.

Language Functions

A. 2. It's possible that I'll have to work late tonight.
    3. There's a chance we'll go camping this weekend.
    4. My partner and I could live in Europe in the future.
    5. It's likely that I'll be an English teacher someday.

B. Sample answers:
    1. It's likely that I'll go out with my friends.
    2. There's a chance that I'll go skiing.
    3. It's possible that I'll be a marketing manager.
    4. It's likely that I'll live in Canada someday.

Unit B.3

Listening

A. 2. Where   6. what
    3. would   7. out
    4. been   8. great
    5. has

B. 1. Aren't you   6. listening
    2. Do I know you?   7. meet
    3. Not yet   8. my office
    4. Marketing   9. tell
    5. proposition   10. deal

C. *Sweet-Aid:* now
    Auntie Nell Donuts: me
    Laura's Secret: shine; hair

Vocabulary

A. analyze *V*   proposal *N*
    develop *V*   combination *N*
    appointment *N*   react *V*
    pressure *N* (or *V*)   announce *V*
    criticize *V*   recommend *V*

B. 2. proposal   7. developed
    3. announced   8. analyze
    4. recommended   9. criticize
    5. combination   10. react
    6. pressure

Grammar 1

A. 2. was working
    3. was watching
    4. approached / was approaching
    5. looked
    6. was reading
    7. were laughing and making
    8. were playing
    9. stopped
    10. grew
    11. saw
    12. yelled
    13. stared / were staring
    14. was yelling
    15. started
    16. shouted
    17. went

B. Sample answers:
    1. At 6 o'clock this morning, I was sleeping.
    2. At 9 o'clock last night, I was studying and listening to music.

Grammar 2

A. 2. ~~I wouldn't rather~~   I'd rather not
    3. ~~is preferring~~   prefers
    4. ~~I am prefer~~   I would prefer / I do prefer
    5. ~~Do you rather~~   Would you rather
    6. ~~you prefer~~   would you prefer / do you prefer
    7. No errors
    8. ~~having~~   have
    9. ~~preferred~~   prefer
    10. ~~I'd~~   I would

Grammar 3

    3. shorter than
    4. wider than; bigger, more narrow than
    5. more advanced than
    6. heavier than; less stiff than; more flexible; easier

Language Functions

A. Sample answers:
    1. Oh, really? Why not?
    2. Oh, no. Sorry to hear that.
    3. Oh? Who was it?
    4. How awful! Are you OK?
    5. Great! You must be thrilled.

B. 1. Ah. What did you see?
    2. Oh, no! Why was it so awful?
    3. Oh, really? How did it go?
    4. Really? Why not?

Unit B.4

Listening

A. 2. ~~341~~   301
   3. ~~Mrs.~~   Ms.
   4. ~~someone~~   no one
   5. ~~190~~   119
   6. ~~still~~   no longer
   7. ~~vice president~~   VP
   8. ~~who~~   what
   9. ~~building~~   place
   10. ~~who~~   where
   11. ~~anyone~~   anything

B. 2. moment   5. names   8. lunch
   3. angry   6. memory   9. truth
   4. trouble   7. card   10. lying

C. 2. I'm looking for the office of William Meyer.
   3. MDG Records is on the fifth floor.
   4. First, could you sign in, please?
   5. Can I help you find someone?
   6. And she would be with . . . ?
   7. Take the C bank of elevators to the twelfth floor.
   8. Just a moment. They like me to call up first.

Vocabulary

2. whisper   6. were (you) muttering
3. shouting   7. mumbles
4. hollered   8. whisper
5. was screaming

Grammar 1

A. 2. When I was in college, I used to have very long hair.
   3. When I was in high school, I used to listen to rock music.
   4. We used to play soccer for 3 or 4 hours a day.

B. Sample answers:
   1. I used to play softball when I was a child.
   2. When I was in high school, I used to go to movies all the time.
   3. I used to work part-time during the summer.

Grammar 2

A. Sample answers:
   2. Do you have any idea who Jackie Baker is?
   3. Do you remember what Jackie Baker looks like (or looked like)?
   4. I want to know what the truth is.
   5. Why don't you ask which restaurant they went to?

B. Sample answers:
   2. I'm going to find out how he got injured.
   3. I don't know what her real name is.
   4. I have no idea where she went.
   5. I wasn't sure why she wanted to meet me

Grammar 3

Sample answers:
   2. someone/somebody   5. everything
   3. anyone/anybody   6. anyone/anybody
   4. someone/somebody

Language Functions

A. 1. doubt   4. think
   2. trouble   5. certain/sure
   3. know

B. Sample answers:
   2. No doubt about it. The pictures prove it.
   3. Oh, yes. We absolutely need to develop other forms of energy.
   4. I'm not so sure. I think the money would be better spent on the poor.
   5. I'm positive. Most scientists accept it for a fact now.

Unit C.1

Listening

A. 1. there's no Jackie Baker
   2. look
   3. Have a look
   4. right
   5. Do you follow soccer
   6. No

B. 1. I can do   3. never even heard
   2. Could I speak   4. as bad as

C. **Michelle**
   plum-colored
   beige
   blue denim

   Liz
   black
   sky
   gray; long
   oversized

   Shanika
   gray; knee
   simple beige
   black shoulder

Vocabulary

2. h or f
3. c or d
4. d
5. b or e or j
6. g or a
7. i
8. e or a or b or f or j
9. f or e or j

Grammar 1

2. was leaving; realized
3. walked; was eating
4. bought; returned; were eating
5. was watching; called
6. invited; told

Grammar 2

Sample answers:

2. **Amy:** Do you mind if I tape record your family stories?
   Grandmother: No, not at all.
3. **Dean:** Can I use your toothbrush?
   Nick: I'd rather you didn't.
4. **Roshawn:** Could I take you and your sister out to dinner?
   Dean: Sure. Go ahead.
5. **Ms. Boyd:** May I work on a different story?
   Tony: I'd rather you didn't.
6. **Elisa:** Is it OK if I send Talia a card?
   Tony: Sure, go ahead.

BONUS

Sample answers:

1. Is it OK if I leave a little early today?
2. Can I borrow your eraser?
3. Do you mind if I show up a little late?

Grammar 3

A. 3. Dean is stronger than Roshawn.
   4. Roshawn can't lift as much weight as Dean.
   5. Roshawn's college grade point average was as good as Dean's.
   6. Roshawn isn't as popular as Dean.
   7. Roshawn doesn't receive as many fan letters as Dean.

B. Sample answers:
   1. I'm not as talented as Kyoko. She's more talented than me.
   2. I'm more relaxed than my sister. She's not as relaxed as me.

Language Functions

A. 1. Do; do
   2. if; Be
   3. May; didn't
   4. Let; anyway
   5. help; I'd appreciate it

B. Sample answers:
   2. **Couple:** Is it OK if we sit here?
      You: Sorry, but I'm saving these seats for my friends.
   3. **Other person:** Do you mind if I read this?
      You: No, go ahead.
   4. **Other person:** Do you need a hand?
      You: It's all right. I've taken care of it.

Listening

A. 1. for   4. on
   2. up   5. behind
   3. on   6. with

B. 1. seen her around   4. took me to
   2. ran into her   5. She should get
   3. tried out for

C. **Summer Sling smoothie**
   1 sliced papaya
   2 cups of vanilla yogurt
   1 cup of crushed ice

   Avocado Dream sandwich
   3 slices of Swiss cheese
   4 slices of avocado
   2 slices of tomato
   4 slices of cucumber
   1 tablespoon of prepared salsa

Vocabulary

2. catch up on   7. look into
3. Hold on   8. trying out
4. Go ahead   9. comes up with
5. fallen for   10. looks up to
6. breaking down

Grammar 1

2. catch up on   6. go along with
3. end up with   7. give in
4. show up   8. drop out
5. work out for   9. turn out for

Grammar 2

2. to arrive
3. to wait; to find out
4. not to pick
5. choosing
6. not to let; looking into
7. naming
8. looking

Grammar 3

A. 2. Before the month ends, something big will happen to you.
3. After you listen and ask questions, you will know the truth.
4. Your life will be richer as soon as you learn who you can trust.
5. Your friends will say many things about you while you are away.
6. As soon as your troubles are over, you will receive many rewards.
7. You will help a friend just when he or she needs you.
8. Until you face the truth, you won't succeed.
9. Someone will impress you when you don't expect it.
10. Just before you make an important decision, you will receive some surprising news.

B. Sample answers:
1. You will find love when you don't expect it.
2. You will meet many friends while you are in another country.

Language Functions

A. 2. If you ask me,
3. do you believe
4. I'm not really sure.
5. What are your feelings about
6. To tell the truth

B. Sample conversation:
Your friend: What do you think of the new superstore that's opening?
You: To tell the truth, I think it's terrible. I prefer small, locally owned stores.

Unit C.3

Listening

A. 1. interesting
2. better
3. much
4. great
5. persuasive
6. disappointed
7. hard
8. convinced
9. honest

B. 1. give
2. won't be
3. went
4. went
5. see
6. lied
7. didn't lie
8. tricked
9. wanted
10. are you going to do
11. going

C. 2. ~~5.4~~ 4.5
3. ~~$1.5 million each year that the Orbits are in first or second place~~ $1.75 million each year that the Orbits win the league championship
4. ~~2.5 percent~~ .25 percent; ~~1.5 percent~~ 1 percent
5. ~~2~~ all
6. ~~will not appear~~ will appear

Vocabulary

2. out of the blue; out of sorts
3. out of control; out of the question
4. out of work
5. out of place
6. out of the way
7. out of date
8. out of this world

Grammar 1

A. Sample answers:
2. to see if she wanted to watch a video
3. to kill time
4. to go home
5. to attend an international news conference
6. to get ready for work

BONUS
To save time!

B. Sample answers:
1. I changed jobs 10 years ago to have a more flexible schedule.
2. Last week, I went to Chicago to visit a friend.

Grammar 2

A. 1. do
2. have
3. must not
4. 've got
5. don't have
6. has; don't
7. doesn't have
8. had
9. have to

B. 2. F   3. T   4. T   5. F

Grammar 3

A. 2. disappointed/frustrated; disappointing/frustrating
3. exhausting; exhausted
4. interested; bored; boring
5. confused; confusing
6. shocking/surprising; shocked/surprised
7. disgusting/shocking; disgusted/shocked

B. Sample answers:
1. I was disappointed by last night's game. It was disappointing because my team lost.
2. I was confused in my English class today. The grammar point was confusing.
3. I was exhausted after my trip last week. It was exhausting because the plane ride was so long.

Language Functions

1. **Tony:** Do you need me to do anything?
   Elisa: Yes, I really need you to help me with this.
2. **Talia:** It's essential for me to finish this work today.
   Amy: What do you need me to do?
3. **Coach Haskins's assistant:** Is there anything you need me to do?
   Coach Haskins: It's really important that I send these documents to *Newsline*.
4. **Talia:** I've really got to think of a good idea/I've got to think of a really good idea.
   Claire: Do you need me to do something to help?

Unit C.4

Listening

A. 2. 've been working
   3. 've been having
   4. have not let; down

B. 2. f   5. b   8. a
   3. h   6. d   9. i
   4. g   7. e   10. c

C. 2. C   5. N   8. N
   3. C   6. C
   4. C   7. C

Vocabulary

1. hand in
2. leave (anything) out
3. passing on
4. kick (you) out; dreamed up
5. let (you) down
6. figure (this) out; clear (that) up
7. turns up
8. pulled (it) off

Grammar 1

A. 2. has been living; for
   3. has been avoiding; since
   4. has been seeing; for; since
   5. has been calling; since

B. 1. called; was probably sleeping
   2. you've been going; is having
   3. Do you like; I've been admiring
   4. have you been dating; I'm not dating
   5. Were you making; made

Grammar 2

2. Can you clear it up
3. Would you help them out
4. pick them up
5. let them down *or* let us down

Grammar 3

A. 2. the most improved
   3. the most original
   4. the coolest
   5. the most laid-back
   6. the best
   7. the biggest
   8. the most valuable

B. Sample answers:
   1. Junko is the smartest person in the class. She learns very quickly.
   2. Jose Miguel is the funniest person in the class. He always tells great jokes.
   3. Kerem is the most creative person in the class. He has very interesting ideas.

Language Functions

2. In other words, she doesn't want to go out?
3. Are you saying that you're firing me?
4. You mean I'm not on the team anymore?
5. In other words, you don't want to go anymore?
6. You're saying that we can't get home tonight?